Great Hunting Stories

Steve Chapman

HARVEST HOUSE PUBLISHERS
EUGENE, OREGON

GREAT HUNTING STORIES
Copyright © 2010 by Steve Chapman
Published by Harvest House Publishers
Eugene, Oregon 97402
www.harvesthousepublishers.com

Library of Congress Cataloging-in-Publication Data
Chapman, Steve.
Great hunting stories / Steve Chapman.
  p. cm.
ISBN 978-0-7369-2814-4 (pbk.)
  1. Hunters—Fiction. 2. Hunting stories, American. 3. Christian fiction, American. I. Title.
PS3603.H3743G74 2010
813'.6—dc22

                                                              2009053460

Printed in the United States of America

16 17 18 19 20 / BP-SK / 13 12 11 10 9

To the kindred spirits of the hunters
who will read this book.
May God give you many
safe and successful seasons.

Acknowledgments

A heartfelt thanks to Harvest House Publishers for encouraging me to pen the stories in this book. And a special thanks to editor Barbara Gordon for adding her expertise to these tales.

✦ CONTENTS ✦

✦ ONE ✦

BEAR ATTACK!

When Les and his 16-year-old son pulled out of the driveway in the fully loaded family Suburban and headed toward the main road, they waved goodbye to Kathy, standing alone on the front porch of the house. As Les' wife and Brent's mother, she tried hard not to let her worry show. Her husband and teenaged son were going to be venturing into the rugged Montana mountains armed only with bows and arrows while pursuing black bears. Concern for their safety clawed her heart, but there was an abiding hope that something more might be obtained in the wild than just bear—especially for Brent.

The previous two years had been tough for the boy. Though gifted as a learner, his frail frame and quiet demeanor opened him to ridicule from some of the students. A few bullies focused on him, casting cutting and hurtful comments his way frequently. The hurt chewed through his tender spirit like bear's teeth. And the more emotional blood he shed as a result of the word wounds, the more the predators circled, taking quick nips while awaiting opportunities for vicious bites. On more than one occasion Brent came home emotionally battered and bruised.

This academic year wasn't going any better. By early October, Kathy could see the stress in her son's face and the despair in his eyes. He'd endured just about all he could. Attempts to solve the issues via the authorities at the school weren't yielding results, and, in fact, often created more problems.

Even though Brent might encounter danger in the Montana mountains, it was a different kind. Kathy knew he needed a break from the emotional harassment at school. And since Les had been wanting some concentrated hunting time with Brent for quite a while, this seemed like a great opportunity to give Brent much-needed down time and a supportive time with his dad.

Kathy turned and walked back into the house. As she closed the door she whispered, "God, Les is so excited that he's going hunting with Brent. Please give them a great trip and a life-changing journey. Bring them back to me safely, and if You will, bring them back changed for the better—both of them."

Twenty-two hours and what seemed like a half-ton of fast food later, the towering mountains of Montana could be seen through the windshield of the Suburban. As they crept closer to their destination, Brent felt excitement and nervousness building up regarding the hunt. Whether it was because of the awesome size of the mountains or the fact they were going to hunt predators, he was feeling a bit anxious. It was also his first trip to the land of dark timber and his maiden voyage into the woods as a bow hunter.

Earlier that summer his dad had finally convinced Brent to put aside his favorite book for a couple of hours and go to Phillip's Archery Shop with him for an evening of friendly competition. For Les it wasn't just a time to enjoy the company of other archers gathered to engage in a little ongoing rivalry. The event also offered a surefire way to ensure that his muscles stayed tuned for the movements bow shots require during hunting season.

Brent had quietly sat on a bench behind the firing line and watched the participants. As he focused on his dad, a figure appeared before him with a half-dozen field-tipped arrows in one hand and a compound bow in the other.

"I'm Ed Phillips, the owner of this place. You're Les' son, right?"

"Yes, sir." Brent's brief answer was delivered with a reserved and awkward tone, but it didn't sway Mr. Phillips from his quest.

"Well, while your pop is trying to outshoot his buddies, how about trying your hand at this archery thing tonight, young man? We have one open lane, and I have a bow for you that should work great. It has a peep sight and a first-class setup. What do you say? Want to give it a fling?"

Brent hesitated for a moment and then stood up. "Sure. Why not?"

Les couldn't believe his eyes when he happened to look down the shooting lane and saw his normally reserved son accepting the challenge to nock his first arrow. As he waited to return to the firing line, he watched his son receive a quick-shot technique tutorial from Mr. Phillips. His heart raced with excitement that his prayer that Brent would discover an interest in shooting the bow might be answered. His hopes were high, and he held his breath as Brent stepped to the line and came to full draw. It seemed like forever before he let the first arrow fly.

The aluminum shaft went straight and the arrow made a familiar *fwap* sound as it hit the paper target mounted to several layers of fiberboard 15 yards from the shooting line. Amazingly, Brent's first shot had pierced the target inside the thin ring that surrounded the ten spot. Les was thrilled to see where the arrow hit, but that sight was no comparison to what he saw when his eyes shifted back to the shooting line. There was his only son uncharacteristically smiling from ear to ear as he received congratulatory pats on his back from Mr. Phillips. Maybe a bow hunter was being born this night!

Brent looked down the shooting lanes toward his father and their eyes connected. Les saw a huge grin, a yes nod, and an excited expression that said, "Now I know why you like this place, Dad!" That assumption was confirmed when Brent gave his dad

a thumbs-up. He then put his hand out toward Mr. Phillips for another arrow.

Brent's second shot hit just left of the first one and above the bull's eye about five inches—but well inside the outer edges of the 11 x 14 paper target. As Brent nocked another arrow, it was all Les could do to hold back tears of joy. He felt a wellspring of thankfulness that Mr. Phillips had issued an archery invitation to Brent.

"Hey, Les!"

Les looked toward Mr. Phillips.

"Hang your bow on a nail and come over here!"

Mr. Phillips didn't have to say it twice. Les walked toward lane one, his heart pounding with excitement. He was witnessing the birth of a new archery buddy *and* a new era in his relationship with Brent.

"Les, I don't think I've ever seen a young man with a more instinctive leaning for the archery shot than your boy has. His form seems to be as natural to him as breathing." Mr. Phillips turned to Brent and challenged good-naturedly, "Show your pop what you can do, young man."

With a surprising air of confidence, Brent snapped the bright-orange arrow nock onto the string, placed his index finger above the nock and his middle and ring fingers below it, carefully pulled the string back toward the right corner of his lip, took aim, and released it. The arrow flew true and smacked the paper between the other two.

"Hot dog!" Les exclaimed.

Some of the other archers had paused to watch, and they clapped at Brent's success. Les beamed.

During the summer, Les was elated when Brent took the state's bow hunter's safety course. After more practice, Brent had accepted his dad's invitation to go to Montana to hunt bear in the fall. Now

they were on their way. As Les drove along enjoying reliving the steps that had led up to this moment in the westbound lane of the Interstate, his thoughts were suddenly interrupted.

"How much farther, Dad?"

Les heard two distinct emotions in Brent's question. He could tell his son was excited about the hunt that would start the next morning, but he also sounded a little tentative with the reality that they were only a night's sleep away from it.

"We're about an hour from the hotel. We'll check in, get some supper, and go over the topography maps again. You'll love this territory we're going into. I've been there three times. You're in good hands with me, buddy. We'll be fine. And we'll never be more than 100 yards apart during the hunt." Les hoped his confidence would settle his son's apprehension. He decided to add an extra measure of encouragement to help that cause.

"Brent, I've watched you destroy the 10 spot many times at the range over the summer with your bow. And the 3-D targets are worn out in the heart areas from your shots. Like Mr. Phillips said, you're a natural with the bow. You can count on that ability plus the skills you've developed to serve you well out here. I believe if you get a chance to take a shot, you'll do just fine."

"Thanks, Dad. I guess I am a little nervous...and excited!"

"Hey, son, if hunting wasn't a rush and didn't test our nerves, why would we bother to go into the woods? You're ready! And even better, since you've got all your schoolwork done already, we can put our minds in bear gear and concentrate on the hunt."

Brent's smile was more carefree as the tires of the Suburban hummed closer and closer to their destination.

Les silently lifted a short prayer to heaven: "Lord, please bless my son with an opportunity for a bear—and a steady hand to take advantage of it!"

The sunrise the next morning was spectacular. After a two-hour

climb, the men were enjoying it from the mountain. Perched on a huge rock that jutted out from the hillside, father and son waited patiently for enough light to search the nearby meadows using their binoculars. They sat quietly, enjoying the view for 20 minutes, and then Brent broke the silence.

"This is awesome, Dad! I had no idea what kind of view we'd have from up here. This is a little different than our state. I think we should call Mom and have her pack up everything. Let's move here!"

Les chuckled, putting the rubber rims of the binoculars up to his eyes. "I fully agree, son. But it would be best if you made the call. Your mama might accept the idea from you quicker than she would from me."

Both guys searched the high country.

"Well, son, I'm not seeing any bears, so let's hike up a little higher. There's another spot where we can do some glassing, and I've seen bears from there before."

An hour later Les removed his pack and sat down behind a huge tree that had fallen down. He rested his elbows on it for a steady look through his binoculars. Brent followed suit, and the two of them swept the open areas.

"Hey, Dad. What's that in the meadow on the far right? A cow?"

Les pulled his binoculars away from his face to see which direction Brent was looking, and then he put the glasses to his eyes and searched that area.

"Whoa! That's not a cow. That, my good buddy, is a bear. Good eye. You've just found us a beast, and from its size it's probably a male—a boar! He's huge!"

Brent felt a surge of satisfaction that he'd spotted the first bear on their trip. "What now?"

"We get our packs on our backs and go after him! That's 'what

now.' This is great stuff for our first day out, especially since we only have three days to hunt. It'll be a tough hike, but I suspect that meadow is full of something that bear likes to eat. If we don't waste time, we hopefully will get there before he pays his tab and leaves."

An hour later sweat poured off the two hunters as they gasped for air and hurriedly dug the toes of their boots into the steep terrain. The ascent to where the bear was thought to be wasn't an easy one, but they managed to make it relatively quickly. As they approached the meadow, Les gave a signal to stop, hunker down, and listen.

"Brent, if the bear is still here, we're probably about 300 yards from him. I want you to stay right here. I'm going to move closer to the edge of this meadow and take a peek. Keep your eyes on me. I'll wave when it's a good time for you to come closer. Bears don't see all that well, but when you come to me, stay low and be as quiet as you can. Their ears and noses are really sharp. Right now the wind is in our favor, but it could shift anytime. If it does, we'll have to back out and go around to the other side. Keep your eyes on me, okay?"

Brent nodded, swallowed hard, and settled down on his knees to wait. He watched his dad duck-walk toward the open area ahead of them. The lay of the land didn't allow Les to get a full view of the area until he was a little higher. In fact, he would reach the edge of the field before he'd be able to get a clear look.

With his bow tethered to a sling and draped over his back, Les crawled on all fours toward a Volkswagen Beetle-sized rock. Before he stood up to take a look over the rock, he motioned for Brent to make his way up the hill. A few minutes later the two of them squatted side by side as Les quietly coached his son on what to do next.

"I'm going up to that rock about 30 yards from here to see if I can see the bear. If he's there, I'll motion you to come over. Go ahead and nock an arrow in case he's close. Be quiet and stay low as you come up."

Brent could hear the unbridled excitement in his dad's voice and felt the infectious effect of it. His heart was beating as fast as a hummingbird's. He was shocked at how much he was loving the challenge. He quietly cheered his father on toward the boulder.

When Les reached the rock he slowly stepped up on a low mound, stretching to peek over the top of the boulder.

Just as he peered over the top of the rock he realized the swirling breeze had shifted, possibly carrying his scent to the monstrous critter that hopefully was on the other side.

Suddenly, only nine yards away, the bear stood on his hind legs and aggressively growled, staring straight at Les!

Man and beast were in a stand off. Knowing a bear can charge at 30 miles per hour, Les quickly backed down and turned toward Brent. With respectful fear in his eyes, Les desperately motioned for Brent to move back to safety.

Les backed downhill quickly, watching for the bear. The hunter didn't see the stump until his right foot was caught and he tumbled backward. Just then the bear came around the rock. Alert, sniffing, and growling, it purposely moved toward him.

The older man quickly wrestled with the pepper spray can attached to his belt, frantically trying to unclip it as he heard the crunching of leaves and snapping of branches that announced the bear's approach. Knowing he was easy prey for the startled and unhappy beast, Les rose up on his knees and waved his arms while yelling at the top of his lungs, "Get out of here! Yaaaaa yaaaaa! Get out of here!"

The bear halted seven yards from Les and stood upright again. The huge body appeared to be 20 feet tall from Les' on-the-ground perspective. Not good. In the next few seconds Les was amazed at how many thoughts went through his head. *Will Brent get away safely? Kathy's not going to want to get this news. God, have mercy on me...and Brent!*

Suddenly he heard the telltale sound of collapsing bow limbs off to his left. As though in slow motion, he saw a flash of white and neon-green fletching sink deep into the bear's ribs in the lung area. Instantly the monster dropped to all fours and ran off, moaning in pain. Les couldn't believe his eyes. He shot a glance back toward Brent and saw he was scrambling to remove another arrow from his bow-mounted quiver and nock it onto the string.

Les looked in the direction the bear had escaped to make sure he hadn't decided to come back for another round. The beast was nowhere in sight. After 20 or so long seconds of reassuring himself that he was safe, Les sat down, emotionally exhausted. He watched as Brent approached quickly, his mechanical release still attached to the string of his bow. He stood over him like a protective soldier guarding a wounded comrade.

"Son!" Les heaved a huge sigh. "Brent, thank you! Thank you! I can't believe what just happened! What a nightmare!"

"Well, Dad, if you're dreaming, I wish you'd wake me up. I'm shaking all over—and I'm not sure I'll ever stop."

"Brent, do you realize what you just did for me? You saved my life! And probably yours too. How did you have the nerve and presence of mind to get to full draw just now?"

Brent, still in his ready-to-shoot-again stance, looked in the direction the bear had run and answered, "I really don't know, Dad. But I wasn't about to let that bear have you for lunch. I did what I had to do."

With legs that were weak, Les forced himself to his feet and assured his son that the bear wouldn't be returning. Then he said, "Boy, it's time for a bear hug—the human kind!"

As father and son embraced, Les placed his open hand on the back of Brent's head and pulled it to his shoulder. He held him tightly in heartfelt thanks, embarrassed to reveal the tears streaming down his face. Crying wasn't something Les was used to doing in front of anyone, especially another male—even if it was his son.

Brent's heart filled with gratitude that he'd been able to keep his focus and accomplish the task set so suddenly before him. His

eyes also filled with tears as the two men shared the most emotional moment they'd ever had together.

After a full minute of a tight, arm-in-arm embrace, Les pulled back and put his hands on the shoulders of his wet-eyed son.

"Son, I've hunted since I was a kid, well before I was your age. I was 10 when I started going to the woods with my Uncle Travis. I've seen a lot of unbelievable accomplishments by hunters in my time, and I've been in the woods with the best of them. From that 14-point elk your Grandpa has hanging on his wall to the Dall Sheep Uncle Travis bagged when we hunted in the dangerous and slippery high country of Alaska, I've witnessed amazing things. But what you did today tops them all. You showed the most poise in the face of grave danger that I've ever seen."

Brent looked at the ground, an embarrassed but hearty smile on his face as he took in his dad's heartfelt praise. This was his first experience with the not-so-common sensation that overtakes a man when he hears another man talking from the deep region of his heart. He enjoyed the affirmation and approval mixed in with his dad's words. He raised his head to hear more.

"Brent, I don't know how you did it. Today you reached way down inside and found the courage and calm to save my life. I have a feeling you didn't know you had those qualities, and I pray you'll remember where they came from. When I could almost smell that bear's breath and count his teeth, thoughts passed through my head that were things a man thinks about just before he goes to meet his Maker. I was scared for me, but also for you and your mom. When I heard the smack of bow limbs, my fear was interrupted. And then I heard the thud of your broadhead finding the bear and saw the fletching sticking in the bear's side. Your shot was right on the money! I was delivered from death. Son, God used you today in a mighty way."

Les noticed that Brent's eyes were wide as he took in every word. He looked like a lost traveler who had just been saved and was getting nourishment for the first time in days.

"There are a lot of giants in the world that are not any different than that bear," Les continued. "They're sort of like Goliath—you know, the giant young David killed. They want to take you down and devour you and the people you love. Today you've discovered you can defeat them. You have the courage and strength inside you, Brent. You proved it to me and to you. On this Sunday morning, right here on this great cathedral mountain, God showed you He is with you. He knew you were ready and worthy to be tested! And I'm sure glad you passed!"

Les was gently squeezing his son's shoulders and felt them relax. He knew his words were finding his son's heart.

"Son, I'm not sure if this is the best time to mention this but I'm going to go ahead while the windows of our hearts are wide open. I know you've been badgered by bullies at school. I feel sorry for them now because they don't know who they'll be facing next Wednesday when you get back. The truth is, those kids are pitiful, and they've obviously never had anyone show them how to treat people and why they should be considerate. They need help. It might be tempting for you to use your newfound confidence to take some revenge, but that's not what those boys need. I urge you to be brave enough to love them and pray for them."

Brent's lips went straight and his jaw muscles tightened, but gradually his face relaxed and understanding shone in his eyes as his dad's logic took hold.

"And I'm sure you're not the only target of their insults. The best way to deal with this situation is to respond quietly but firmly, pray for them, and, if you see someone being attacked by them, stand beside that person and bolster his or her courage. Your friendship with their other victims could very well make those cowardly predators run."

"I'll be honest with you, Dad. And this isn't easy to say. I've rehearsed all kinds of insults to use to get back at those guys, but none of them ever seemed strong enough. About a month ago I started thinking hitting back would be better. Then I realized they'd gang up on me and I'd lose again. The next step seemed obvious. I should use some kind of weapon. Bullets would certainly work better than words. In my mind I imagined firing as many rounds as the times they've hurt or embarrassed me."

Les' eyes were wide and his mouth tight as he studied his son. He removed one hand from Brent's shoulder and waited for more information.

"Dad, that's not going to happen now. I promise. Not after today. This trip has changed me. Thank you for bringing me with you. I don't like being hurt…and I sure didn't like the thought of hurting anyone because I know how it feels. But I didn't know what else I could do. Now I have an inkling. I'm telling you now, on this Sunday morning, on this great mountain, that those guys are not going to hurt me ever again. I won't let them do it anymore. I'm going to try what you said about responding firmly, praying, and putting up a united front with other kids being bullied. For the first time in a long time, I can't wait to get back to school!"

Les put his open hand on the side of his son's head, and gently said, "I'm proud of you, Brent. You are 'da man,' and I mean that from the bottom of my heart! And if you ever get frustrated and hurt to the point where you think about resorting to violence, come to me. I won't judge you negatively, and we'll work together on what you can do about it. Okay?"

"Okay, Dad. Thanks. I appreciate that."

"Now, Brent, we need to get back to business. That bear is out there, probably mortally wounded. We need to find it."

As the two men hefted their packs onto their backs, Brent's chest swelled with the assurance that he was greatly loved by his dad. He smiled as he realized how great he felt…and it seemed to go to the very core of his being. Self-doubt had been erased in the last 20 minutes. His steps felt more sure, his hearing seemed more keen, the air on his exposed skin felt crisper, and his eyesight seemed

to pick up more of his surroundings. Confidence flooded his heart and soul. He felt terrific.

Less than 10 minutes later the invigorated hunters found Brent's momentous kill collapsed next to a downed tree. After making sure the animal was dead, they attached the carcass and hide tags and spent the next few hours field dressing the bear and removing the cape. They talked and laughed as they labored over the beast, and by early afternoon they were making their way down the mountain packing the heavy hide and two game bags full of meat. They stopped often to rest and relive their morning's adventure. Each time the story was rehashed, more details came to light, making the telling even more dynamic and dramatic.

When they reached the Suburban and loaded the meat and hide into the oversized coolers they'd tied to the hitch-mounted tray, Les proposed a change of plans.

"Brent, I don't know about you, but I'm not sure I can wait until Tuesday to tell your mom about your adventure…and I'd sure rather show her your trophy instead of just telling her about it on the phone. Why don't we go straight to the checking station, report this kill, and then head east? We can get some of the trip under our belts this evening, find a hotel, and then finish it tomorrow."

"Are you sure, Dad? You haven't filled your bear tag…but I'm sure looking forward to telling Mom and my friends about this hunt!"

"Yep. I'm tuckered out with all the excitement. And your mama's probably worried about us. You've bagged enough bear meat to last us a while. And most of all, I want to see your mother's face when she sees this cape and hears what you've done. The sooner that happens, the better."

"Okay, Dad! Let's head home. Do you think we should let Mom know we're coming home early?"

"We'll call her when we get up tomorrow to complete the drive. We'll give her ample notice, but I'm not going to tell her the details

of why we decided to head home so soon. I'll let you do that when we get home. Deal?"

Brent smiled. "Deal!"

Kathy heard the Suburban roar into the driveway just before sundown on Monday evening and ran out to meet her men. As they hugged and said their hellos, she noticed Brent's excited smile and Les' big grin. "You guys look like the cat that swallowed the canary," she said. "What's up with you two? And don't try to hide anything from me. You know that's not possible!"

Les cleared his throat and gestured for Kathy to join him and Brent at the rear of the Suburban. The two guys lifted the two coolers off the metal hitch tray, opened the one that contained the cape, and took it out. As they unfolded it, Brent was sure his mom's eyes were bigger than fried eggs as she realized the size of the pelt and saw the head.

"My word, Les and Brent! That thing is huge! Who got this beast?"

Les grinned and glanced at his son. "That's the look we gave up two days of hunting and drove all those hours for, buddy! Was it worth it?"

Brent, an ear-to-ear smile distorting his face, answered, "Sure is!" He turned to his mom. "I got this one, Mom!"

For the next half hour Kathy stood next to the vehicle and listened as her son and husband talked about their dramatic hunt. They interrupted each other to fill in details, and when they got it all out, Kathy asked them to repeat their tale. She was speechless and kept shaking her head in awe and relief as the story unfolded again.

Finally the story was told and retold, and the men returned the hide to one cooler and toted the meat-filled one into the garage for butchering and packaging later that night. They would take the hide to show Mr. Phillips and then have it tanned and mounted by a local taxidermist.

As Les and Brent unloaded the Suburban and put away their gear and supplies, Kathy noticed a difference in her son. His quick, sure steps and squared shoulders revealed a new confidence and self-assurance. Even the tone and pitch of his voice seemed stronger. And best of all, he was sticking close to his dad as they worked side-by-side in companionable silence. Suddenly the prayer she'd said right after they'd left for their hunting trip echoed in her mind: *Bring them back to me safely, and if You will, bring them back changed for the better...both of them.* Gratefully she acknowledged God's answer. She knew Brent had turned a corner and would be okay.

That night, after their son was settled in his room for a night of deserved and peaceful rest, Kathy went to the garage to help Les wrap up his chores. As her husband cleaned his hands, she said, "Les, I'm thrilled you and Brent could share the hunting experience you had. But if I'd known what your trip was going to entail, I would've done my best to keep you both here. I'm so glad God was watching over both of you!"

Les rolled his eyes a bit and smiled slightly, debating whether to share that if he'd known what was going to happen maybe he'd have stayed home without a fight.

Kathy shifted from one foot to the other, a movement she always made when she wanted to continue talking without interruption.

"Of all that you and Brent told me regarding that bear, the one thing I haven't heard about is how this experience has drawn you two together. I can see there's a new bond between you. Brent followed you around this evening like a real buddy. The change is obvious to me, and I wanted to make sure you noticed it too."

Les nodded his head in humble agreement.

"And, sweetheart, there's something even more astounding that took place while you and Brent were in Montana. I saw it as plain as can be this evening."

"What's that, Kathy?"

Kathy moved in and put her arms around her husband's waist. She softly and confidently said, "Les, you took a boy to the mountains…and brought home a man."

Les looked toward Brent's bedroom and then lowered his gaze to his wife. With moist eyes and a gravelly voice he whispered, "I guess so, honey. I suppose we both changed…for the better. Thanks for letting us go."

TWO

SEASON OF CHANGE

E d placed his thumb firmly on the fully cocked hammer of his .30-30 and carefully pulled it back slightly. After putting slight pressure on the trigger he eased the hammer forward, all the while watching the nice six-point whitetail that had been in his scope for nearly five minutes. As the deer fed across the field from his left to right and toward the tree line Ed pushed the safety button to white and whispered, "Count your blessings, Mr. Young Buck. If this had been 20 or 30 years ago—or shucks, even 5 years ago, I would have laid you down before you got 10 yards into this field."

Ed lowered the rifle to his lap and continued watching the lone deer until it moved into the shadowy woods. As he turned his attention back to the four-acre field he was hunting, a feeling he'd encountered only a couple of times in recent seasons came over him. The first time it happened was two years ago. A sizable seven-point appeared within rifle range on a drizzly January morning. When he found the deer in his scope and rested the crosshairs on its lung area, he pulled the hammer back and took a deep breath. He exhaled and was just about to pull the trigger when he realized something was missing in the shot process. His desire to take the buck lacked its usual intensity. Though he sensed the excitement of being in that special moment when everything that needed to happen to get a good shot had fallen into place, he knew the inner

fire for the kill had lost heat. As the buck browsed on the acorns that were plentiful that year, Ed mentally assessed the thoughts that surprised him.

> *What's going on here? Am I getting soft in my late fifties? Am I getting lazy and don't want to do the work that comes after the shot? I know I'm healthy enough to get that deer to the truck by myself. With the limit they've put on us for one buck, this could be my only chance this year, and he's plenty big enough to take. If I'm gonna do it, I'd better be doin' it now. That buck is not gonna be here all day! So… whatever's got me hung up, it's high time to deal with it and either squeeze the trigger or ease the hammer down.*

Convinced that his hesitation to take the shot was some sort of melancholy that would float away in the breeze with the wisp of smoke his .30-30 would create when fired, Ed slowly pulled the trigger and watched the buck drop where it was standing.

His emotions seemed back to their normal high as he retrieved the deer, field dressed it, and dragged it to his truck. Like all the years before, it felt very satisfying to report to his hunting buddies that his efforts had yielded success. All was well again. Until the next deer season came anyway.

Another opportunity to fill his tag walked within 30 yards of his tree stand. When the buck stopped and stood at an angle perfect for a lung shot, he'd slowly raised his rifle to his shoulder and found fur in the scope. But just like the year before, he felt resistance to pulling the trigger. This time it seemed even stronger.

During the 20 or so seconds the crosshairs were on the deer's vitals, he tried to convince himself that the real reason he didn't want to pull the trigger was that the deer wasn't the size he wanted. He argued, *Besides, there is plenty of season left to find something bigger and heavier.* Though they were good reasons to let the deer walk, he knew there was a deeper cause for his hesitation. With the rifle

back in safe mode and the buck browsing nearly out of range, Ed shook his head in bewilderment and sighed deeply. *Something is just not here…not like it used to be anyway.*

As that second season progressed, Ed opted to pass on more chances to take deer. In the mid-December section of gun season, when he noticed that the inventory of venison in his freezer had gotten low, he responded to the need to refill it by taking a very healthy-sized doe. He was grateful for the meat, but he was also very excited about being excited when it came time to take the shot.

From time to time Ed thought about the somewhat flattened emotions he'd felt when the chances for shots came in the previous years. Finally, after mulling it over, he came to a life-changing and important conclusion. He realized the thrill of the kill was no longer his primary motivation for hunting, and that a very real shift in drive had taken place. Though taking the shot was still an undeniable emotional rush, he knew the next time he had the chance to make a kill he would likely feel more apt to do it if it was "purpose driven," a phrase used quite often in his church. Whether it would be to fill his freezer or another family or friend's, Ed found welcomed comfort in resolving the issue. If he took another deer, he would need a reason to do so beyond matching wits with the wary deer. He was grateful to know that if an opportunity to take a deer did present itself and he decided not to pull the trigger, he would at least have a better understanding of why.

In this third season of again facing the challenging truth that he'd just refused to take a legal deer, he pondered again the stage of life he was in as a hunter. Though he'd come to grips with the change and was glad he wouldn't be surprised by it in the future, he still couldn't help but wonder if the youthful, climactic rush of seeing a deer, taking the shot, and watching it go down would be something he'd feel again. A tinge of sadness came over him as he sat quietly by the empty meadow.

He carried that melancholy, along with his unpunched deer

tag, for the rest of the season. Now he was in his fourth season of "the attitude change," as he called it. Around late August when the first signs of fall appeared, Ed started looking ahead to the coming season, but he reluctantly admitted that his fervor for the hunt was still weak. He doubted if the enthusiasm would return to the level he'd once enjoyed. But he was going to go out into the woods anyway.

November came. On a Sunday morning just six days before the opening morning of deer season, Ed declared "amen" with the rest of the congregation at the end of service, picked up his hat, and headed to the foyer with his wife. As they stood in the hall making small talk with a few friends, a lady in her mid-thirties approached him.

"Mr. Carson? Do I have the right person?"

"Yes, but you can call me Ed."

As they shook hands, the younger lady continued. "Ed, my name is Kate, and I've been coming to this church for a little over three months now."

Ed smiled. "Yes, I've seen you around. I apologize that we haven't met before. I'm not too outgoing, as you've probably guessed."

Kate returned an understanding smile. "I'm a single mother, Ed. My husband was killed at the Thompson River Bridge construction site about four years ago."

"I remember that accident—a fall, I believe. I'm so sorry."

Kate fought the emotion that was still raw and went on. "Thank you. It hasn't been easy, but I'm doing okay. My son is too. In fact, he's the reason I'm talking to you. I've heard you're an avid hunter."

"You could say that, Kate." Ed tried to conceal the sudden satisfaction he felt that came with the unsolicited title, even if he had doubts about the "avid" part.

"My husband loved to hunt. At the time he died, he was looking forward to taking our son, Jason, to the deer stand with him. Because Jason was a little too young to go when his dad left us,

he's not yet had the opportunity. I'm way too busy trying to make ends meet to take him, and I really don't know the first thing about hunting anyway."

As Kate talked, Ed began to see what was coming. His excitement was obvious when he asked, "How old is Jason now?"

"He's 12. He turns 13 in a few days...just before deer season opens. I know he'd love to go. Sometimes I find him sitting and staring at the 10-point buck his dad got and had mounted the year before he died. It hangs on the wall of our den. Jason has talked and hinted over and over again about wanting to do what his dad enjoyed so much. A few months ago we went through the hunter's safety course. Bless his heart. He had to put up with me being pretty much in the dark about most of what was taught. Now he can legally hunt, but it didn't work out for him to go hunting with any of the hunters teaching the course. He's pretty bummed about it. So that's why I looked you up, Mr. Carson...er...Ed. I know it might be an inconvenience, but would you consider taking Jason hunting with you sometime this year?"

Ed's knees nearly shook as joy rocked his heart. He looked at Kate with a fatherly expression and said, "You have no idea how happy I'd be to take Jason to my deer stand this year! How about next Saturday morning? Opening day? Just tell me where you live, and I'll pick him up about two hours before sunup. Jason and I will go huntin'!"

"Thank you!" Kate shook Ed's hand.

He saw tears forming in her eyes as she said, "He's already got the outfit to wear!"

Ed couldn't control the chuckle that came with the words she used to describe her son's hunting clothes. It was a sure sign the boy could benefit from some males in his life.

"Does Jason have a gun he can use?"

"His dad used a...let's see, how did he refer to it? A .30-06."

"That's a big gun for a young hunter. If it's okay with you, I'll

let him use my old .30-30. That's a perfect rifle for a beginning hunter."

"That sounds great, Ed. Thank you!"

Kate wrote down their street address for Ed and thanked him again for agreeing to take her son to the woods. She turned and headed down the hall toward the youth department.

Ed turned back to his friends to continue their conversation, but he really didn't hear a word anyone was saying. In his mind he was working on how to make a wider seat in the homemade, wooden ladder stand where he and his new young friend would be sitting in a mere six days.

Saturday morning came way too slowly for Ed and Jason. But finally it arrived, bringing along a very clear sky and cool, crisp weather. The lights were on at Kate's house when Ed pulled his pickup to the curb. When he knocked on the front door, Jason opened it, fully dressed in camouflage, good heavy boots, and a thick heavy coat that looked a little too big for him.

"Good morning, Mr. Unseth. I'm Ed Carson."

"Good morning, sir. And you can call me Jason."

Ed looked at Kate and smiled. "A hunter and a gentleman. I like that. He's a sharp one, Kate."

"You're right about that, Ed. Is he dressed well enough for hunting in this outfit?"

Jason rolled his eyes and then very politely reminded his mother, "It's hunting *gear*, Mom."

"Oh yeah, hunting gear. I need to remember that."

Ed spoke up. "Looks to me like you've got all the gear you need for a chilly morning, Jason. You might want to take the coat off until we get to the farm we'll be hunting."

Kate shot a concerned look at Jason as he cleared his throat. She knew what he was about to say.

"If you don't mind, Mr. Carson, I'd like to keep the coat on. It was my dad's."

Ed silently wished he'd discerned that detail before he suggested Jason remove the coat. The wave of emotion that came from hearing the reason for the boy's determination to keep the coat on was powerful.

"No problem, young man. I just meant that you don't want to be too warm in the truck so that when you get out the cold will feel even colder. We'll just roll the windows down on the way to the farm so you won't get too hot. It'll be good to get used to the cold early anyway."

Jason smiled and tried not to look like he was lunging for the door, but his excitement and determination to get going was getting the best of him.

Kate stepped up to herd the two hunters outside. Suddenly she stopped. "Oh! I almost forgot to send your lunch with you, Jason." Kate grabbed a well-stuffed plastic grocery bag off the counter. "There's enough food in there for you too, Ed, just in case you're out past noon."

"Thank you, Kate. That's mighty kind of you. Speaking of time, deer hunting is not a totally predictable thing. We might get into something right after daybreak or we might have to walk around and stir something up. I plan to have Jason back by two this afternoon though. If we get a deer early, we'll spend the rest of the time scouting."

Jason looked at his mother as he smiled and opened the door. He quickly translated what Ed had just said. "Scouting is when you look around for deer sign and learn what areas they favor and where they're moving and stuff."

Ed grinned and looked at Kate. "Yep, he's a sharp one all right. He's on target with his understanding of what scouting is all about. And really, scouting is half the fun."

As the two hunting companions walked out of the house and across the porch, Kate said, "You boys be careful now. And thank you...God bless you, Mr. Carson." Kate's eyes glistened with unshed tears.

Ed turned and waved. Then he smiled down at Jason, patted him on the back, and glanced at Kate. "I have a feeling we're gonna have ourselves a good hunt today, Kate!"

Jason climbed into the cab of the truck, closed the door, looked down the sidewalk toward his mother, and waved.

Ed took his coat out from behind the truck seat and put it on, anticipating the cold ride ahead. He climbed in behind the steering wheel. As he started the engine and lowered the windows halfway, he said, "You sure have a nice mom, Jason."

"I sure do, Mr. Carson. And I sure love her for letting me go with you today. And I sure appreciate this hunt."

"You're more than welcome, Jason. You have no idea how excited I am about this day. It might be hard for you to believe, but I just might be more pumped about going hunting than you are."

Jason laughed. "No way!"

On the way to the 180-acre farm the two would hunt on Ed did most of the talking. Over the roar of the chilly wind whipping through the half-opened windows, Ed gave a quick lesson about the lay of the land and the possible directions the deer would come from...if they showed up.

"These deer haven't been hunted much, except by a couple of bow hunters. And they don't hunt the place very often so the animals aren't very skittish yet. The field we'll be hunting is one of their favorite feeding spots in the morning and evening. I'm kind of thinking that they very well could be there pretty soon after sunrise. We should spot them...that is, if we're quiet enough going in."

With the low, white glow of the dash lights Ed could see his young friend's eyes were wide with the excitement of possibly being in shooting range of a deer. To paint a realistic picture of the unpredictability of deer hunting, the seasoned hunter quickly and intentionally deflated Jason's hopes a little by adding, "Don't forget, there are lots of does on this farm, but we need bucks. We're not as fortunate as other hunters in some of the other states where taking a buck or a doe is legal during gun season. And keep in mind that when I talk about seeing a 'shooter buck,' I'm not talking about a spike. We're looking for ones with some age on them—meaning visible antlers. We want the very young ones to have a chance to grow in size."

Jason responded to the idea with a more mature attitude than Ed expected.

"Well, since I've never seen a deer while on a deer stand, just seeing some whitetails will be fun for me," the boy asserted.

Ed smiled at the thought that his young partner was showing such a positive attitude. "We'll be at the farm in about five minutes. Before we leave the truck and walk to the stand, I want to go over firing the rifle you'll be using this morning. Have you ever shot a high-caliber rifle, Jason?"

Jason straightened up in his seat and fidgeted a bit. "No, sir. Is that a problem?"

"Absolutely not," Ed said. He could see the relief in Jason's eyes and face as he relaxed. "I think you'll find my old .30-30 very friendly to first timers. The kick is very mild. In fact, you might not feel it at all if there's deer in your sights."

"Oh, I'm not afraid of a gun. I've had a BB gun for quite a while. I know it's nothing like what you use, but I love the feel of a gun in my hands. I've never used a scope though."

Ed pulled the truck up to a cattle gate at the farm entrance and parked. "We're here and in plenty of time to pack up and be on the stand before the sun rises. As far as using a scope, the one thing you'll discover is that it's tough to keep the crosshairs steady on a target if you don't have a solid place to steady your aim against. Shooting free-handed takes some practice. I have a 'shooting rail' built on the stand we'll be using that will help you make a good shot. Now I'm going to leave the headlights on so I can show you the rifle."

They got out and met at the front of the truck, Ed cradling a soft gun case in his hands. "This one is a beaut! I've gotten quite a few whitetails with it."

Jason's face lit up when Ed slid the .30-30 lever-action out of its case and handed it to him.

"You probably learned this during the hunter's safety, but the first thing you should know about a gun is that if someone hands you a weapon, whether a rifle or pistol or whatever, you always point the shooting end away from anyone standing nearby. The next thing you do is check to see if it's loaded. A fellow told me once, 'Even if Jesus hands you a gun and says its not loaded, check it anyway.'"

Jason laughed and looked expectantly at Ed.

"Well, truth is, Jesus is the *only One* we should believe if He says a gun is not loaded. For all others, double check and see for yourself. First of all, never put your finger on the trigger until you're ready to fire the gun. Understood?"

Jason answered, "Yes, sir."

"Okay, now make sure the safety button is on. It's right there near the trigger. See the white ring? That means the safety is on… that it's in 'safe' mode. See it?"

"Yes, sir. I see the white."

"Now, put your right hand inside the lever and push down with the back side of your fingers near your knuckles to open the chamber and check to see if there are any bullets inside. You might need to shift position so you can use the headlights of the truck to see clearly inside the gun."

Jason followed Ed's instructions and confidently responded, "No, sir. There are no bullets in this gun."

"Very good, Jason. Now pull up on the lever to close the chamber. Put your right thumb on the hammer spur—that piece that protrudes to the right off the hammer. Pull it back just a little until you hear it click."

Jason looked up at Ed when he heard the click. "Did I do it right?"

"Yep. That's what you listen for. Now the gun is in a 'half cocked'

position. With the safety on, even if the hammer gets pulled back accidentally and was released, it won't hit the firing pin.

"Okay, now put the gun up to your shoulder and look through the scope. Can you find the half moon in the sky? When you do, put the cross hairs on it."

"Cool! I can see the moon, Mr. Carson. The lines are really thin, but I can see where they cross."

"Good. Notice how hard it is to keep the crosshairs on one spot while you're holding the rifle to your shoulder."

Jason peered through the lenses for about ten seconds and said, "You're right. If the moon was a deer, I think the critter would be pretty safe with me shooting this way."

Ed enjoyed Jason's clever humor. "Once daylight comes and we can see some distance from the stand, I'll show you how important using a rest can be. Maybe—just maybe—the first time you lay a rifle on the rail to steady a scope it will be to take a shot at a deer!"

Realizing he had probably inflated the boy's hopes along with his own, Ed continued the lesson. "I want you to put the gun back to your shoulder and point it toward the field beyond the gate. Once you have it settled, put your thumb on the hammer spur and press down firmly."

Jason followed the instructions with surprising confidence. With his thumb in ready position he waited for Ed to go on.

"Pull the hammer all the way back until it engages. Don't let go of it—keep pulling back until you hear it click."

With the hammer cocked, Ed reached up and put the tip of his forefinger on the safety button on the side of the gun.

"Once you get the hammer back, you push this button in with your finger. Remember, when you can see the white on the button on the right side of the gun, you're on 'safe.' When you push this button all the way in, it comes out the other side and shows red. That tells you that the gun is in 'fire' mode. This is a critical detail, so make sure you remember."

Jason looked away from the scope and said, "My BB gun has something a little bit like this. Daddy told me the same thing. You can be sure I won't forget about it."

Joy mixed with sorrow flooded Ed's heart as he heard Jason's reflection on his days with his dad.

"Your papa taught you a very valuable lesson, Jason. And I'm proud of you for remembering it."

Jason's quick smile and subtle nod revealed how good it felt to hear a man aim the words "I'm proud of you" at him.

"Okay, now I want you to put your forefinger on the trigger. Slowly pull the trigger back. As you do, relax a bit and let the falling of the hammer surprise you."

The click of the hammer hitting the firing pin made Jason smile.

"That's how it feels to fire this rifle—minus the boom, of course. And that's how simple it is. I know this is a quick lesson, but we'll talk more about it when we get on the stand. Would you like to carry the gun? We'll load it when we get there."

As if cradling an infant, Jason wrapped his arms around the .30-30 and nodded.

Ed gathered the rest of the gear. He transferred the packed lunch to a canvas bag that wouldn't be so noisy opening when they got hungry. Turning, he led the way across the cattle guard.

"We have a 10-minute walk to the field where we'll hunt. Stay behind me, and I'll point my flashlight down so we can see where to step. We need to be quiet as we go, so let's not do any talking."

Not another word was exchanged between the two hunters until they reached the tree that had a tall ladder stand leaning against it. Ed whispered, "I'm gonna go up first. When I get up top, I'll drop a thin rope down that has a clip on the end. Attach it to my gun's sling, and I'll pull it up. Then I'll drop it down and you attach your gun to it. When I give you the word, you climb on up. I'll hold the light so you can see what you're doing."

The two hunters settled in on the elongated chair of the stand. As the sky gradually changed from black to a pale blue-gray, Ed spoke with a breathy voice as he shoved five cartridges into the loading port of his .30-30. "It's a little dark to show you how to load and unload your gun so I'll show you later. Here's your loaded gun. You're all set. Now I want you to listen with me. In just a few minutes, if you keep your ears tuned in, you'll hear some birds wake up and start to sing. Not long after that you'll probably hear a crow or two cawing. If there are turkeys in the area, they'll wake each other up with some yelps. This is nature's orchestra, and there's no prettier music in the world...except maybe the crunch in the leaves that says a deer is walking nearby."

Ed watched Jason cock his head sideways as he listened intently so he wouldn't miss one note of the concert. All at once Ed realized the anticipation on Jason's face was a reflection of the excitement that had suddenly returned to his own heart. The sage hunter looked toward the field that was becoming more visible. He smiled deeply.

"Was that a crow I just heard?" Jason asked in his best whisper.

Ed peered carefully across the field and slowly answered, "Actually, that was a blue j..." He stopped mid-word and gently elbowed Jason. "I want you to slowly turn your head and look at my eyes. Figure out where I'm looking, and then look that way. I see two deer coming into the field from the left side about 80 yards away."

Jason followed Ed's orders and responded tremulously, "I think I see 'em, but they're sort of fuzzy. What do we do?"

"We need to wait for more daylight. It's not legal to hunt until a half hour before sunrise. Let's hope the deer feed long enough to let us figure out if they're bucks."

"Do binoculars work in this kind of light?"

Ed was so excited about hunting with his young partner and seeing the deer in the field that he'd completely forgotten about the binoculars hanging on a lanyard around his neck.

"Very good question, Jason." Ed slowly raised the glasses to his eyes. "Brilliant question, in fact."

Jason beamed.

Ed studied the two deer carefully through the binoculars and then announced, "They're both does. Lean toward me and look through these glasses."

As Jason located the two whitetails in the binoculars, he was physically close enough to Ed that the older hunter could hear the boy's breath quicken. He could almost hear the boy's heartbeat! The excitement was infectious, and buck fever hit Ed's soul, rekindling a fire he'd feared had been permanently doused.

As the daylight grew and legal shooting hours arrived, Ed caught sight of movement at the edge of the field, just beyond the browsing does.

"Jason! There's another deer coming into the field," Ed whispered. "Look to the left. It's standing at the edge of the woods. Can you see it?"

"Oh! Mr. Carson, I see antlers!"

Jason's leg started bouncing.

"Watch your leg, Jason. You need to quiet your body to keep movement noise to a minimum. Deer have excellent hearing. Steady now. You've got a job ahead of you in the next minute or two that requires calm and focus."

Jason breathed deep and asked, "Am I going to shoot at that deer?"

The words that floated softly out of Ed's mouth were the same words he'd heard 40 years earlier when he was hunting his first deer. This time they seemed even sweeter. "He's yours. Take him!"

Jason was nearly paralyzed with excitement, but he managed to focus. "What do I do? Please tell me what to do!"

Awakening from his reverie of his first hunt, Ed briefly shook his head to help him pay attention to what was at hand. "Lift the rifle as slowly as you can. Rest the barrel on that wooden rail. Put

the stock firmly against your shoulder and point the muzzle toward the deer. Lean slightly forward. Tilt your head and look through the scope, but make sure your face isn't resting against the scope. Tell me when you find the buck in the crosshairs."

Ed's heart raced as Jason followed his instructions.

"There he is, Mr. Carson! I've got the crosshairs on him. He's just standing there looking around."

Ed fought for more air as he gave the next instructions. "He's standing broadside, so I want you to find the top of the front leg with the crosshairs. Then come up about halfway to the top of the back. Now move the crosshairs toward the back of the buck just a little."

"I remember this from the safety course. I'm sure I'm aiming at the heart area."

Ed took a deep breath and exhaled.

"Do this with me, Jason. Take a deep breath and exhale."

Jason's shoulders rose and fell.

"Now, if you have the crosshairs steady and solid on the heart area, I want you to pull your eye away from the scope, look at the hammer, and put your thumb on it firmly."

The buck took a few steps toward the two does and stopped.

"Jason, pull the hammer back. Don't let the pressure off until you hear it click. We're too far from the deer for them to hear it if you do it gently. When the hammer is engaged, don't put your finger on the trigger yet. Look through the scope and find the buck again. He's moved about ten yards further into the field."

"I have him. I have the crosshairs on his rib cage. Now what?"

"Push the safety button to the 'fire' position. Okay. Softly put your finger on the trigger."

"Okay."

Ed felt his blood throbbing through his jugular and was sure pure adrenalin was flooding his arteries. "Make sure the deer is standing still, and then pull the trigger when you're ready. I'll be watching the buck through the binoculars."

Five long seconds passed and then Jason fired.

Even though he expected it, the blast made Ed nearly jump out of the stand. He steadied the glasses and saw the deer kick high with his hind legs. He knew Jason's shot had connected as he followed the deer's labored jumps into the trees.

"Great shot, Jason! I believe you've got your buck! In fact, I'm absolutely sure. I saw him go down just inside the timber. You got him, young man!"

Ed quickly lowered his binoculars and reached out to shake Jason's hand.

In the same instant, Jason threw his hand in the air for a high five. The boy quickly lowered his hand to shake Ed's hand just as Ed adjusted for the high five. They both laughed at their fumbling with the congratulation ritual and finally completed both gestures.

Ed's heart pounded and he felt a rush of energy surge through his body. The fire for the hunt had roared back into a full-blown blaze. "Jason, I am really proud of you. You did a great job. You were born to do this, little buddy. You're a natural!"

Jason's shoulders relaxed, and he silently stared at the floor of the tree stand for a few seconds. He shifted his focus to the downed buck.

Ed finally broke the silence. "Don't deny what you're feeling right now, Jason. Embrace it! Take it in! Tell me how you're feeling. I want to hear it."

Jason struggled to answer as his throat caught and tears welled up in his eyes.

Not sure if they were tears of joy or tears at the magnitude of taking a life, Ed searched for just the right words to say.

"My Dad called me 'little buddy,'" Jason cut in. "I wish he could be here to see this."

The dam of reserve broke in Ed's heart, and salty tears ran down his face. He put his arm around Jason's neck and pulled him into his shoulder. He was surprised at how small Jason's body felt in the

large, heavy coat. "Jason, I choose to believe that your dad didn't miss a thing this morning. In fact, I'm kind of thinking that just maybe he's inside that coat you're wearing...inside your heart. Right now he's saying, 'Little buddy, you're amazing!'"

Jason's lips parted as he smiled and rubbed his eyes.

"Now it's time to go get your deer." Ed dug for his hanky and muttered, "Thank You, Lord. The fire for the hunt burns again!"

"What do you mean, Mr. Carson?"

Ed smiled as he wiped his cheeks. "I'll explain it to you later, Jason. We need to get after that deer." He looked at the boy. "And by the way..."

"Yes, sir?"

"Is that coat keeping you warm enough?"

"Oh yes! I'm happy to be in it."

Ed pushed the button on his flashlight. "I'm sure there's someone watching right now who is happy you're in it too."

→ THREE ←

THE
HIDEAWAY

Dan raised his head and sat back, stretching out his arms. He'd been plowing through piles of documents stacked on his desk and needed a break. His secretary entered his office, a serious look on her face.

"Dan, your wife is on the line. She says it's urgent. It's about your brother." The secretary turned and left his office, shutting the door on her way out.

Dan swallowed hard as he searched for the phone hidden under the mountain of papers and folders. He fought the dreadful possibilities that tore through his mind. He found the phone and put the receiver to his ear. Pushing the button that was lit, he said, "Yes, Claire. What's going on with Jimmy?"

"Dan, Angie just called. She's on her way home from going to the doctor with Jimmy. They just found out he has pancreatic cancer." She paused.

The silence was finally broken as Dan heaved a big sigh. "God, please have mercy on us…on Jimmy. Oh Claire, that's something I hoped I'd never have to hear. And he's five years younger than me. Where is he right now?"

"He's driving home behind Angie. I can't believe they'd let him drive after getting such devastating news. I can't imagine what's going through his mind right now."

Dan stood up and switched the phone to his other ear. He turned

and looked out his office window. He was on the fifth floor, and the city spread out before him. While he searched for words, tears formed in his eyes. They felt like acid as they spilled onto his face. Sadness and long-ignored guilt hit him hard.

Pancreatic cancer was one of the most vicious and swift thieves of life. And Jimmy had it. Regret stabbed his heart. He hadn't spent much time with Jimmy in the last few years. The relentless require- ments necessary to keep his advertising business afloat, his "can't say no" responses to requests to be on community organization boards, his active role in his church, the sometimes overwhelming responsibility of being sole provider for his family of four, and the energy and effort required to maintain their home had built a wall between the two men who used to be so close in heart.

Dan's thoughts were interrupted when he suddenly realized Claire was still on the line. "What, honey? Um…I need a minute to think. In fact, let me wrap things up here quickly, and I'll head home. We can talk about this more then. Okay?"

"Okay. Drive carefully. I love you, Dan."

"I love you too." Dan slowly turned, placed the phone receiver in its cradle, and then faced the window again. He stared at the maze of buildings and the busy streets below. As he wiped away his tears with the back of his hand, he imagined his brother driving down the highway. He pictured Jimmy sitting behind the wheel of his pickup. *What would someone think about after learning the 30 or 40 years of living he'd assumed he had left might be gone?*

Though he wished he could be in the truck cab with his younger brother, Dan knew his brother was exactly where he'd want to be. Jimmy had always preferred to be left alone for a while when life dealt him a challenging hand. While some people might run to people for solace when hardships arose, he always seemed to do better if he could first disappear to a private place, confront his thoughts and feelings, and pray a while. After he did that, he usually emerged ready to deal with reality head on.

He learned that from Dad, I bet. How did that Bible verse go that Dad was always quoting when difficulties arose? Oh yes—Luke 4:42, "At daybreak, Jesus went to a lonely place." Dan smiled as he recalled the mischievous inflection in his dad's voice when he used that verse as leverage for going to the woods during hunting season. *"Even Jesus needed some quiet time!"*

The memories of his dad faded, and Dan looked eastward, toward his brother's house 500 miles away. His mind drifted back to a December day more than 25 years ago. The smell of fresh, frigid air, the blanket of pre-Christmas snow on the ground, and Jimmy rushing out the back door flooded his senses. The two brothers were running out to unleash their beagle and hit the brush in search of rabbits.

"Jimmy! Slow down, kid. We've got all morning. Mom said Aunt Sarah won't get here until one or two o'clock."

"Why do we have to be here when Aunt Sarah comes, Dan?" Jimmy complained.

"'Cause Mom said so. I don't want to hear all the gabbing about Aunt Sarah's friends and the clubs she belongs to either. Who cares about that stuff? But we don't want Mom mad at us the day before Christmas."

"Okay, Dan."

"We have plenty of time to hunt. Let's make the most of it."

"Bob the Beagle," a long name for a short and stocky dog, was jumping wildly on his hind feet while clawing at the wire fence with his front feet. Jimmy lumbered swiftly but clumsily toward the pen, and Dan laughed as his 11-year-old brother nearly fell on the slick snow by the chain link gate as he rushed to open it.

"That dog can feel a hunt coming a mile away. He can see it in your eyes, Jimmy. He knows he's about to hit the brush with you. You two are just alike."

Jimmy and Bob the Beagle seemed to be on the same wavelength.

When they'd adopted the pup two years before, those two had bonded immediately. Dan was convinced the only thing both of them thought about night and day was chasing rabbits. Not being as keen on rabbit hunting as those two, Dan didn't mind that he wasn't part of their little world. Besides, being the oldest he had plenty of other interests. Right now he accepted his role as watchman and protector over his rambunctious brother and the high-spirited beagle. And since Jimmy loved to shoot his single-shot .410 shotgun, being his "brother's keeper" was an important assignment, especially because their dad had died of cancer five years before.

A knock on the door startled him. Dan turned around. "Come in."

"Is there anything I can help you with?" his secretary asked.

"No thanks. I just got some bad family news, so I'm going home early. If anything comes up, you can call me there."

"Okay," she replied. This time she left the door open on her way back to her desk.

Dan threw a few folders into his briefcase and grabbed his coat. He left his office, said goodbye to his staff, and headed outside. He got into his car...and just sat there, his mind going back to that day so long ago.

White vapor clouded in front of Dan as he repeated the dog and safety instructions that were standard fare before each rabbit hunt. "Jimmy, you gotta keep Bob on the leash until we get beyond the barns and close to the creek. Don't let him go till we jump something, and we're sure it's a hopper. We don't want him chasin' a deer. And don't load your shotgun until you know Bob's on a rabbit scent. Remember, don't pull the hammer until just before you're ready to take the shot. You got all that?"

"Got it, Dan!" Jimmy shouted as he ran behind Bob. When they got near the high grass and patches of briars that lined the creek,

Dan had to double-time to catch up. Just as he arrived at the water's edge, his brother yelled.

"There he goes, Dan!"

A startled cottontail rocketed away from the sudden presence of dog and humans. It shot through the underbrush as Jimmy quickly dropped to a knee to unhook the leash from the dog's collar. In his haste and excitement he fumbled with the metal clip. Bob the Beagle's excited jumps as he dug his claws into the snow-covered ground and fought to start the chase didn't help either. Finally the dog and leash were separated. Jimmy clenched Bob's collar and led him to where he'd last seen the rabbit. Jimmy let go and hollered his favorite command: "Go get 'im, boy! Hunt 'im out!"

Bob the Beagle hurled through the brush, nose close to the ground.

Dan had stopped to watch the starting ritual. He hollered, "Jimmy, did you put Bob the Beagle on the trail where you last saw the rabbit? If you did, he'll do the huntin'. He'll run the rabbit in a circle, bringing it back toward you."

Jimmy stood, turned, and shot an aggravated look at Dan just before he rolled his eyes.

Seeing Jimmy's irritation at being reminded of something so obvious, Dan shrugged his shoulders and lifted his arms in an "I'm sorry" gesture. When Jimmy nodded, Dan mimed the "don't forget to load the gun" gestures.

Jimmy's body stiffened as he clenched his teeth and frowned. Suddenly he looked at his gun, glanced quickly at Dan, reached into his pocket, and pulled out a shell that he immediately loaded into the shotgun.

After the breakdown gun was closed, Jimmy looked at Dan with a smile, confessing his forgetfulness and thanks with a casual "come over here" wave.

Dan stepped quickly to Jimmy's position and stood a few feet

behind him. He was tall enough that he could see over his brother's head.

They both watched for movement in the underbrush.

Jimmy's near whisper filled the air. "Why didn't you bring your 20-gauge, Dan?" Jimmy already knew the answer because he'd been asking the same question for nearly two years.

"I want you to have all the fun, Jimmy."

"Okay. Don't move around and mess this up."

Dan smiled at Jimmy's youthful-but-authoritative command and wondered how his baby brother had become such a hunter. *Jimmy was probably born with the instinct to chase rabbits,* he decided. *Just like Bob the Beagle was.* Being told to stand still and not booger up the hunt didn't faze Dan at all.

When they both heard Bob approaching and letting out a series of short, high-pitched yelps, they knew he was hot on the rabbit's trail. Jimmy stood quietly, the stock of the .410 resting on his hip. The barrel was pointed upward and his thumb rested on the hammer.

Suddenly Bob the Beagle broke into the glorious beagle anthem that happened every time the fresh and pungent aroma of rabbit filled their nostrils. Dan wondered what lyric was pouring from Bob's soul until he heard Jimmy.

"Listen to that, Dan! Don't that singin' sound good? Bob's tellin' us, 'Get ready, boys. I'm bringin' this critter to you!' Sing it, Bob the Beagle!"

Dan struggled to control his laughter as the beagle's solo echoed through the field that lined the creek. Though he couldn't see him in the tall grass, the dog's baying was easy to track. By the sound, Dan knew the chase was heading back their way. He knew the creek would interfere with the rabbit's instinctual preference for a full circle run. When the critter got to the creek bank it would either head down the creek bank or it would bounce through the brush along the water's edge toward them.

In a few minutes the sound of Bob the Beagle's relentless aria

made it obvious the rabbit had turned and headed toward the creek. If it turned downstream, it would probably live to see another day. If he turned right, it was a pretty sure thing he'd face Jimmy's well-honed shotgun skills and their mother's frying pan. Unless, of course, it came upon a rabbit hole to run down.

The moment of truth came. Bob suddenly went silent. For what seemed like an eternity the brothers held their breath and listened. *Did the rabbit drop into its underground hole? Was Bob the Beagle disappointedly staring down a dark hole?* Suddenly another stanza of the pursuit anthem crashed through the brush.

Jimmy turned to his right, put the shotgun to his shoulder, rested his thumb on the hammer, and waited for his shot. Dan stepped to the right, moving a few feet behind his brother. They listened as Bob's bark got closer and closer.

Dan intently watched the thick grass and heavy brush along the bank. When he saw a flash of brown fur shoot between two clumps of frozen grass, he turned to see if Jimmy had seen it. His brother's hand was clenching the shotgun and the hammer was pulled back.

The report of the .410 echoed, followed closely by a sound Dan would never forget.

"Oh no! No…no! Oh, God!"

Dan jumped to Jimmy's side as he suddenly realized his brother's shot had gone wide, missing the cottontail but hitting Bob the Beagle.

Jimmy dropped the shotgun in the snow, buried his face in his gloves, and sobbed his anguished prayer of sorrow and hope.

Dan stepped around his weeping brother and ran to the beagle. By the time he knelt at the dog's side, their pet was taking his last breath.

Dan turned to check on Jimmy, but he was nowhere to be seen. He scanned the area, spotting Jimmy just as he topped a small rise and disappeared down the other side. Dan checked Bob's vital signs once more even though he knew it was a futile gesture. He gathered up the dog, picked up the shotgun, and headed home. He was pretty sure he knew where his brother had gone.

When he neared the house and went over a low hill, Dan saw Jimmy disappear into a thicket on the side of a small hill that overlooked their house. In that tangle of gnarly trees and vines, the two brothers had carved out a fort. It was their private place, but Jimmy spent the most time there. On occasion Dan would join him—mostly when food was involved. They would scarf down a half dozen of their mother's biscuits slathered with jam and stuffed with ham.

Dan stood on the rise and debated whether to join his brother or go to the house and tell their mom what happened. After a minute or two of arguing with himself, he decided to leave Jimmy alone for a while. When Jimmy's emotions were contorted, Dan's attempts to console him and talk to him were usually met with a "go away" followed by stony silence. After bad days at school, unkind comments from friends, or discipline from their mom, Jimmy seemed to fall off the deep end if someone tried to get him to talk. Dan had discovered Jimmy recovered faster when he could work through his thoughts and feelings in solitude.

He turned toward the house, wondering how to tell his mom what had happened.

Their mom was standing at the sink when Dan pushed the back door open and walked into the kitchen.

She turned toward him, saying, "You're home earlier than I exp…" At the sight of his face, she stopped. Turning pale, she rushed to him. "What happened?"

"We were out hunting. Bob the Beagle was hot on a rabbit's trail, bringing the cottontail around to where we were standing by the creek. Jimmy shot at the rabbit…but missed and hit Bob the Beagle. Bob is dead, Mom." Suddenly sadness overwhelmed him. Tears streamed down his face as he struggled to add the details.

"We had a chase going, Mom. It was wonderful. Bob was bringing the rabbit right to us. I saw a flash of fur and heard Jimmy's shotgun boom. Jimmy realized he'd hit Bob before I did. He cried out and dropped his gun. I ran to help Bob, but he died just after I got to him. When I looked back Jimmy was gone. I picked up Bob and the gun and headed home. I saw Jimmy go into our fort.

"Jimmy kept screaming, 'No...no! Oh, God!' He said it over and over. It was awful, Mom."

Dan reached to the table and grabbed a napkin out of a wire holder. He wiped his eyes and nose as his mother gently hugged him.

"Are you okay, Dan?"

"I'm sad about Bob, but I'm worried about Jimmy."

Dan's mother raised the hem of her apron to her eyes and dabbed the tears away. "I'll get my coat and boots." She stood and walked toward the coat hooks and boots by the door. "Where is Bob the Beagle?" she asked.

"I carried him home. He's right outside."

Dan watched as his mom put on her boots and shoes. "Will Jimmy be okay, Mom?"

"We both know how he is. He likes to be alone when he's really upset. But it's cold out there. He'd better come into the house. Hopefully he's had the quiet time he needs. Jimmy and Bob the Beagle had a very special relationship, so this is going to be very hard for your brother—and for us too."

Stepping outside and shutting the door, mother and son headed up the hill toward the thicket fort. As they approached they could hear Jimmy talking inside his domed hideout. Getting closer, they realized he was repeating between sobs, "I'm so sorry, Bob. I'm so sorry." Just before they got to the fort's entrance, Jimmy quit talking. After a short pause they heard him again.

"God, will you tell Bob something for me? Tell him I'm sorry. I didn't mean to hurt him."

Reaching the barrier of briars and vines, Dan uttered their

traditional entrance noise and then announced, "Jimmy, it's Mom and me. Can we come in?"

"Uh-huh." Grateful for the warning "knock," Jimmy quickly wiped his eyes with his sleeve and stood up. Though he was a young boy, he had a man-sized reservation about being found crying. He stepped back and forth to get the blood circulating in his almost numb legs.

Dan and his mother crawled in and gave Jimmy a hug. Nothing was said for a time as a loving mother held her two heartbroken sons close and gently patted each of them on their backs.

"Jimmy, Dan and I are so sorry about Bob the Beagle. And I'm so glad you have this place to go to when the world caves in on you like it did today. Have you talked to God about what happened? This sure is a wonderful place to do it. God knows you didn't mean to shoot Bob. He's not mad at you. And I know it was an accident. So does your brother."

Dan kept his arm around Jimmy as he listened to his mother's soothing voice. While she spoke, he could feel his brother's body slightly relax.

"Boys, it's okay to be sad about Bob. And you'll grieve for a while. That's okay too. And you won't be dealing with this alone. I'm here to talk anytime you want, and I'll be praying for both of you. And you can pray for each other too."

Dan and Jimmy nodded their heads.

Jimmy looked in the direction of the creek, pain visible in his reddened eyes. Then he surprised them. He threw his shoulders back and pursed his lips, a thoughtful look on his face. Then he announced, "I need to go get Bob and bury him. I want to do it here by my fort."

"That sounds good, Jimmy. Dan carried Bob the Beagle home for you. He's by the back door. I'll get a blanket and wrap it around him."

Before long Dan and Jimmy had pick-axed through the frozen

ground just inside the hideaway and prepared a resting place for their dog. With that accomplished, the only thing left to do was go to the house and get Bob's body.

Jimmy knocked the dirt off his gloves as he spoke firmly to his elder brother. "I'll go get Bob. I want to do it alone if you don't mind."

Dan took issue with the idea but didn't succeed in lending his brother a hand. He did step outside the fort to watch Jimmy as he headed downhill to the house. Tears still trickled down his cheeks. For a minute Dan wondered if they'd ever stop.

When Jimmy got to the house, he went directly to the blanket-wrapped bundle by the back door. He stood there for a while before bending over and picking up the dog. He carried him up the hill to the fort and placed him gently in the grave. Both boys covered Bob the Beagle's body with dirt.

The service the two boys had for their furred friend was short and agonizing. Then Jimmy asked Dan to leave. Knowing his little brother needed more time in his hideaway with Bob, his feelings, and his prayers, Dan left willingly. In fact, he never went back to that spot on the farm.

Through the years Dan knew Jimmy went to the secret fort when he needed solitude. Jimmy even mentioned a couple of times what a great place it was for his "altar." A plastic, five-gallon bucket turned upside down served as Jimmy's pew. And no place of prayer anywhere on earth—even the gilded and massive cathedrals in Europe—were a match for the simplicity and serenity in this little haven.

As Dan drove across town to be with Claire, he continued to think about Jimmy and the drive he'd make back to the home place tomorrow. Although both boys had inherited the property when their mom passed away, Jimmy and his wife, Angie, were the ones who lived there.

When he got home Dan put his briefcase in his home office, hung his coat in the closet, and then found Claire. After a brief hug and short conversation, he called Jimmy and Angie.

"Hello."

"Hi, Angie. This is Dan. Claire told me the news about Jimmy. I'm so sorry. You and Jimmy have been heavy on my heart this last hour or so."

Angie thanked Dan for his concern and filled him in on the details of the visit to the doctor's office.

"Has Jimmy gotten home yet?" Dan asked when Angie finished.

"Yes. He insisted on driving himself home. You know how he is when he's upset."

Dan nodded, forgetting Angie couldn't see him. Then he said, "Yes, I know how he is. He's still following Jesus' example about the 'quiet place' rule. Will he speak to me?"

"He's not in the house right now. He wasn't home but five minutes when he walked out the back door. I'm guessing he's up in his hideaway. Someone else called about 15 minutes ago, and I hollered for Jimmy, but he didn't answer or come in. I'm debating how much time I should give him before I start worrying."

"Angie, I'm sure you're right about where he is. Give him an hour or two." Dan's voice was thick and gravelly. "When he gets back to the house, he'll be easier to talk to. Will you ask him to call me when he gets in? And if it fits with Jimmy and your plans, Claire and I'd like to come down there for a couple of days."

"That would be great," Angie replied. "We'll be here."

"Good. Tell Jimmy I'm coming down to do a little hunting with him. And let him know I'm bringing my old 20-gauge. He'll understand."

"I'm sure Jimmy will look forward to that! Thank you for calling, Dan. I'll let Jimmy know you want him to call you back. He's going to be so glad when he hears you and Claire are coming down."

FOUR

PETE'S PRAYER

Pete's breathy whisper was as low in volume as he could possibly make it and still be heard by his friend next to him. "Don't move a muscle, Lenny. There's a huge gobbler coming down the edge of the field to my left. He's gonna walk right in front of us. When his eyes go behind that big tree, that's when you can get your gun up to your knee."

Lenny felt the torturous ache in his rear end from sitting so long and quietly. He complained quietly to Pete, "I can't stay in this position much longer."

"You can wait," Pete prodded. "The tom is almost behind the tree. Wait…wait. Now! Move your gun up!"

Lenny quickly raised his weapon and lowered his cheek to the stock. He took careful aim to the right of the tree. His breathing quickened and his pulse raced. The world around him disappeared except for his gun, the tree, and the huge tom that would appear any second.

There he is! Lenny squeezed the trigger and couldn't resist adding his vocal 20-gauge shotgun blast imitation the second his gun fired. A projectile of saliva flew from the back of his throat and hit his teeth before dribbling down his chin.

Pete instantly reacted to Lenny's shot with a victorious, "You got 'im!"

As the boys turned toward each other to do a high five reality abruptly butted in. They froze as they realized 200 or so saints at Wells Grove Church were staring at them. The silence was deafening. Even the people sitting up front and in the choir loft were staring at them, mouths agape.

Shocked, the pastor stopped his sermon mid-sentence.

Only the subdued swooshing sound of material sliding against oak pews filled the hall as the congregation members shifted their bodies to look back and forth between the pastor and the two boys.

The two youthful hunters felt their faces getting warm from the hot glares coming their way. Pete froze, not moving an inch as he took in what was happening as far as eye movement alone would allow. Lenny, still crouched in shooting position with both feet up on the pew, realized he couldn't feel his body. Seconds passed like hours.

Lenny finally looked up, white faced, and stared at Pete.

Fully aware that the turkey that had wandered into their fourth row fantasy hunt was not the only creature that would be suffering that morning, Pete quickly tried to think of a way to survive the incident. He mentally hurried through possible ways to ward off pastoral and parental execution. In the midst of his racing thoughts he noticed Lenny was still holding his mother's umbrella on his knee like it was a shotgun. Very slowly he placed his hand on the flowered, hook-handled, shiny, makeshift 20-gauge and lowered it to the pew.

Pete lifted his head and looked over the benches to the front of the church. The first face he focused on was his dad's. Standing behind the pulpit, the look on his face resembled someone who had just witnessed a horrible car wreck. As disturbing as it was to see his dad's contorted face, it was nothing compared to the expression he saw when he scanned the choir loft's sea of green robes and found his mother. When his eyes met hers, he instantly recognized the similarities between his mother's choir robe and that

of the cloaks judges wore. Pete realized his days of freedom were probably numbered.

Not bearing to maintain the connection with his mother's eyes, Pete looked down. He'd heard sermons about hellfire and brimstone, and he was sure he was experiencing the first signs of them right now. The fiery darts his mom was shooting at him hit their mark. His insides felt like a churning mass of fear. He blinked and hunched his shoulders.

Convinced his life—and likely his friend's—was about to be stripped of necessities such as bicycles, TV, video games, baseball gloves, and ice cream, Pete desperately aimed a prayer heavenward. Suddenly, as though an angel had hand-delivered the thought, he remembered a sermon his dad had preached not long ago. He closed his eyes and puckered his lips as he tried to remember the details. It was about a grand and joyful yet-to-happen event.

What was the word Dad used? Something about future happiness Christians would experience. He searched through his memories, and lo and behold, there it was! Armed with the knowledge, Pete instantly enacted the plan he was sure God had given him. He jumped to his feet, reached skyward with both hands, looked straight up, and with the impetus of desperation let loose a fervent prayer: "Oh, God! Let the *rupture* happen right now!"

Two levels of silence are known to mankind. There's a quiet that is given that name only because it is a lot less than the noise it has replaced. Though called silence, it is really a "near silence." What might be considered stillness in a large room might include slight hints of noises, such as breathing, an occasional soft clearing of a throat, perhaps a creaking pew. The deeper level of silence is not often experienced, so when it is, it's rarely forgotten. This is when a complete and pure hush falls over everyone and everything in attendance.

Pete lowered his gaze to see if the plan had worked. He noticed stunned looks on some faces but quizzical looks on others. *Did*

I get it wrong? he wondered. He waited. His lungs seemed to be working overtime and sweat was beading on his forehead. No one moved. Pete was sure everyone's hearts had stopped beating, and people must have quit breathing because he couldn't hear a thing. Even the candles seemed to stop flickering.

Gradually he heard the sounds of life creeping in. Then he heard something. *What was that? A giggle? Someone is laughing? What's happening?*

The stunned members of the congregation were slow to react, hesitant to be the first to break into the silent moments. At first trickles of giggles broke through the cracks in the dam of seriousness, followed by snickers and then outright nasal snorts. Suddenly the concrete wall of poise burst and a torrent of laughter reverberated through the sanctuary. Knee slapping, floor stomping, pew pounding, as well as some shoulder slapping and gasping from laughing so hard added to the din.

The pastor—Pete's dad—bent over double trying to contain his laughter. He knew there would be no immediate recovery. The only one thing to do as the leader was to let the laughter river roll on for a while.

After a while the room calmed down a bit, and the sounds of deep sighs of relief, nose blowing, and eye wiping with tissues were heard. At that point, the pastor stood behind the podium with his hand on his chest, as if checking to make sure he wasn't experiencing a cardiac episode. He said, "Folks, in all my years of being in church and around praying believers, I've never seen a prayer answered so quickly. A *rupture* has indeed taken place here, and I can still feel it's effects in my aching side."

As it often happens, once laughing starts in a crowd, whatever words follow, even if only slightly funny, rockets up the laughter meter. The volume of chuckles rose again, and the loudest decibel maker stood behind the pulpit. As Pete Sr. stepped away from the solid cherry wood podium that usually evoked clerical seriousness,

he knew he was helplessly in the throes of a laughter breakdown. Fighting for air, he abruptly glanced over at the choir loft to locate his wife. He couldn't find her right away and momentarily worried whether she was headed to the fourth row pew to take care of their mischievous son.

Soon he noticed one of the choir members wiping her tears with the sleeve of her robe with one hand and waving at him with the other. When he focused on her, she pointed to the floor at her feet. There, partially hidden behind the backs of the chairs, was his dignified wife. All he could see was the top of her back. From her movements he guessed she was laughing hard.

Completely unraveled by the sight, Pete Sr. made his way back to the podium and placed a palm on each side to brace himself so he wouldn't collapse from the restricted amount of oxygen he was taking in. Then, struggling for composure, he spoke brokenly to his unglued parishioners.

"For a moment there I couldn't find my wife. I was so afraid she'd been..." He paused to gain some semblance of control and say the next word clearly. "...*ruptured!*"

With that statement came one more tidal wave of hooting and hollering. As the laughter rolled over the congregation again, the people who hadn't been feeling well physically and emotionally when they showed up for service suddenly were feeling much better. There were hard-lined, crotchety stoics of the church who would never dream of letting people act with such frivolity in the sanctuary, but because they were so surprised by the boy's innocent prayer, they too were caught up in the merriment.

While all this was going on, Pete had slithered back onto the pew next to Lenny. They looked at each other, mouths agape, as they took in the unexpected reaction. Pete smiled a bit, interested and surprised by the way his folks were handling his prayerful outburst. Hope seeped in...his prayer may have succeeded!

Look at Dad, Pete thought. *He's lost it. Since he's laughing so hard,*

maybe he won't kill me after all. And Mom…Where is Mom? Oh, there she is. Good grief—she's on the floor. Is she mad? No…no…I think she's…yes she's laughing! A minute ago she looked like she was going to ground me for life. I don't understand why everyone is laughing, but this has to be a good thing. Is this what a rupture is?

"Hey, Lenny, I have no idea what just happened here, but if I'm right, me an' you ain't in trouble."

"My folks are going crazy," Lenny whispered. "Look at them! I don't think I've ever seen dad laugh like that—ever. And Mom keeps elbowing him even though she's laughing too."

"Do you know why everyone is laughing? I don't get it. It's probably good for us though. No one looks mad anymore."

Finally order returned. Pete's dad straightened his tie and stood behind the podium. "That was certainly an unexpected development, wasn't it? In the interest of time, I'm going to table the rest of my sermon. We'll talk more about Paul's teachings next week."

Pete's mother settled back into her choir chair and turned her gaze to her nine-year-old son. She gently dabbed at her wet and red cheeks. She wasn't sure whether she should laugh at Pete's hesitant smile or frown at him for disrupting the service. She could tell he wasn't sure why everyone was laughing and smiling at him. He was fidgeting but listening intently.

"Pete…son…you know I love you. And you are my favorite hunting buddy. Obviously you and Lenny let your imaginations get the best of you this morning. We'll discuss this situation later."

He watched his son nod slightly and look at the floor. He could tell Pete was worried about what was going to happen…and rightfully so. Pete Sr. decided their yard was going to look exceptionally nice by the end of the month.

"Now, about the 'rupture'…I mean the 'rapture,' of course. There were two very important principles in Pete's prayer this morning. The first is knowing for certain that in the last days when Jesus calls us to heaven, each of us will be ready. John 14:1-3 says, 'Let not your

heart be troubled; you believe in God, believe also in Me. In My Father's house are many mansions; if it were not so, I would have told you. I go to prepare a place for you. And if I go and prepare a place for you, I will come again and receive you to Myself; that where I am, there you may be also.' And in the book of Revelation, verse 22:20, John reminds us, 'He who testifies to these things says, "Surely I am coming quickly." Even so, come, Lord Jesus!' Let's live in such a way that we're never afraid, and we can look forward to that momentous day."

With a pastoral gentleness, Pete Sr. wrapped up, "And in today's service we've certainly discovered the importance of a good sense of humor. Proverbs 17:22 says, 'A merry heart does good, like medicine.' We adults often forget that during the stress and busyness of our days. This morning we've been reminded of what a gift God has given us when He wired us to enjoy good belly laughs.

"Laughter decreases stress hormones and increases immune cells. It improves blood flow. Science tells us also that endorphins, that unique feel-good chemical our bodies create, is stimulated by laughing. And shared laughter brings us together, joining our hearts and lives."

Around the sanctuary heads nodded in agreement, and the music director came forward and led them in a hymn. Pete Sr. noticed an increased energy level as people stood for the benediction. He bowed his head and prayed, "God, thank You for how You surprised us at this service with the very welcome gift of laughter. We needed the visit. In fact, some of us feel much better right now than we felt when we came through the doors this morning. Help us share the invigorating medicine of humor with the people we meet this week. In Jesus' name we pray. Amen."

After his prayer, he looked over at the organist and said, "Please play the G note." He turned to the congregation. "You'll know this song the moment we start it."

With a certain graceful perkiness, the lady at the organ raised her right index finger and brought it down confidently on G.

The pastor hummed the note then turned to the congregation and said, "For our benediction, please join me in this familiar chorus by George Willis Cooke:

> I've got the joy, joy, joy, joy
> Down in my heart (Where?)
> Down in my heart (Where?)
> Down in my heart
> I've got the joy, joy, joy, joy
> Down in my heart (Where?)
> Down in my heart to stay."

As 200 voices lifted in festive singing at Wells Grove Church, none of them sang harder or louder than Pete and Lenny. That's what fellows do when their prayers have been answered.

FIVE

I AIM
TO PLEASE

D on set his gear bag next to the ladder-back wooden rocking chair on his front porch as he sat down. He laced up his leather boots as he listened to the muffled sounds of shouting coming from inside the house next door. "What could they be fussin' about at this early hour of the day?" he wondered aloud.

At quarter past four, Don was up to go hunting with his neighbor Phil. The young man and his wife, Marcy, had moved in two years ago, and on a couple of other occasions the audible signs of marital discord had filtered through their walls.

As he finished securing his boot strings Don noticed the new silence. A couple of minutes later the aluminum storm door squeaked open and Phil appeared with his bow case and a bag of camo clothes. As he walked toward his truck that was parked at the curb, his steps were heavy and his head was hanging down. Except for the hunting gear, he could have been going to a funeral.

"Morning, Phil!" Don called as he walked toward Phil's rig. He intentionally added a bit of cheer to his greeting in hopes his young friend wouldn't realize he'd overheard the less-than-happy start to his day.

Phil mumbled, "Hey, Don. You packed and ready?"

"Yep. Thanks for driving this morning. My son insists he needs

the truck today to help his girlfriend haul something. I bet it's a load of hairspray and makeup."

Don's attempt at humor roused only a flustered complaint from Phil as he circled around, opened the truck door, slid the bench seat forward, and stowed the gear behind the seat. He flipped the seat back and climbed in behind the wheel of his huge, eight-cylinder, four-wheel-drive truck.

After Don opened his door and climbed in, Phil replied, "Yeah. Women. When you get 'em figured out, call me."

The two men slammed the truck doors, latched on their seat belts, and Phil turned the key. The big engine roared to life. Phil put the transmission in drive and pulled away from his house, accelerating so quickly that Don's head nearly slammed the window behind him.

Don glanced over at Phil but resisted the temptation to offer fatherly advice about his heavy foot. He searched for something else to say that might slow the street rocket that had just been launched.

"Did you get your bow restrung, Phil?"

"Yep. Picked it up after work yesterday and got it honed in last night at the archery shop. I reckon I was there till nearly nine-thirty."

Don was thankful to hear the engine back off some rpms as Phil talked.

"I can't believe that bow came unraveled like it did. And of all the times! That buck was not more than 15 yards from my stand. I would've had him, Don. Stupid bow."

"How long you been chasin' this buck, good neighbor?"

Phil quickly rubbed his eyes. "I saw that monster in mid-August while clearing out some shooting lanes around my stands. I've only seen him a couple of times since. Now that we're so far into the season without spotting him, and after I educated him about my presence like I did the other day, I'm not sure if I'll ever get another chance. If I don't see him within a few minutes after first light, it

probably ain't gonna happen this morning. That means I'll have to come back out here this evening."

Don heard the frustration in Phil's voice. And hearing his advance plans to return for an evening hunt if no string was released this morning was revealing.

At nearly 62, Don had hunted with enough fellows through the years that he recognized serious hunting obsessions when he saw them. Some of his friends were deeply passionate about the pursuit of whitetail but were the type who could laugh away times when things went right for the deer. However, there were a few of his buddies who took the chase so seriously that they weren't a lot of fun to be around from late September to mid-January. Phil seemed to fall into the latter category, and Don wondered if a little probing might help him understand why…and maybe even help him avoid the unhealthy plunge.

"My friend, that old boy has a hold on you, doesn't he?"

"Yeah, I reckon he does. You don't know how bad I want to plug that critter. And I'll be honest with you, Don. You have no idea how badly Marcy wants me to get it done too."

Don kept his facial muscles relaxed and didn't break into a smile when he realized his prying had generated important information. Phil's subtle admission about Marcy's interest in the hunt implied she might not be all too happy with Phil's hunting strategy.

As the darkness submitted to the first light of another November day, Don and Phil sat in their tree stands that were separated by a tall ridge and about 400 yards of hillside timber. They welcomed the coming sun as their eyes slowly adjusted to the change of light.

Phil was replaying the argument he'd had with Marcy that morning.

Don was trying not to imagine the young couple in the throes of the spat he'd witnessed earlier with his ears. He wasn't being too successful. The images conjured up weren't pleasant as he silently reviewed

what he thought was their dilemma. *Poor Marcy. If she could look inside Phil's brain right now she'd probably find nothing but bows and arrows, binoculars, range finders, scent bombs, tree stands, camo clothes piled up everywhere, and huge deer running around in small patches of woods. I'm afraid the last thing she'd find is herself. She's dealing with a fellow who is saturated with a level of zeal for the hunt that I've not seen in a while. I wonder where that drive is coming from?*

Don paused for a half minute or so and searched his brain for clues to what could be pushing Phil. Nothing specific came to mind. He went on with his quiet musings as he scanned the ridgeline above him for movement. *There's got to be something deeper going on in Phil's life that's got him at odds with Marcy. For sure, he should never let an aggravation about a malfunctioning piece of equipment and a deer that got away generate the kind of word war they were having this morning. I wish I could put one of those tiny cameras in Phil's mind and work it around until I found the reason...*

Don suddenly interrupted himself when he caught a glimpse of something moving against the narrow patches of gray sky visible between the tree trunks on the ridge. "There it is again," he whispered, sure he was seeing a deer.

He reached for the binoculars that hung on a hook attached to the tree. Talking quietly to himself, he put the glasses to his eyes. "Doggone, that's gotta be the huge deer Phil's been seeing. Look at the size of the body...and that rack! It looks like the rocking chair on my front porch. And unless I miss my guess, he's gonna walk over the ridge on the trail that goes right by Phil's stand." Don grabbed his walkie-talkie and turned it on.

Phil's walkie-talkie vibrated in his pant's pocket. He dug for it as his eyes scanned the area. "Yeah, Don. What's up?"

"Phil, I think that monster you've been chasing is about to come wandering by your stand! My estimate is 5 or 10 minutes. I just saw him through the timber near the top of the ridge. If he doesn't get

distracted he's gonna drop down on that trail that runs by your stand!"

Phil's quiet, serious voice answered, "Got it, Don. I'm going dead on the radio. I'll turn it back on in a little bit."

Don put his walkie-talkie back in his pocket and attached his release to his string just in case the buck altered his course. He listened hard for that telltale, dry cornflake crunch in the leaves that would alert him to an approaching buck. Enough time passed that Don realized the buck probably wasn't going to go by his stand. He still felt the jitters that can accompany a possible encounter, even if it was more likely that his neighbor would be the one to have this one. He searched for other deer, watching intently for movement. *If that buck passes under Phil, I sure hope that boy nails it. What a trophy that would be.*

A long 15 minutes went by before Don suddenly felt his radio tickle his leg.

"Tell me about it, Phil. Talk to me!"

Heavy breathing was the response he got. It sounded like Phil had just finished a hundred-yard dash.

"Don, I got into him! I can't believe it. He came within 12 yards and stopped broadside. I was so pumped I thought I'd never get the peep sight on him. I'm telling you, it felt like I was pulling on piano wire. When I released the arrow, he almost went to his knees. Then he shot out of here like a bullet. I know I got him! I can see my arrow, and I think I see blood on the yellow fletching. Don, I did it!"

Phil's enthusiasm arced like an electrical current between them. Don laughed at the thought of what would happen if another hunter got between their tree stands right now. *He'd be fried to a crisp,* he decided.

Don punched the talk button and answered Phil's radio report with a string of well-deserved kudos. Then he asked, "Did you see him go down?"

"No, but I know he's hurt bad. He's gotta be nearby. I'm sure of it."

Don accepted the assessment. "Unless I have something come by me I can't pass up, I'll pack up in about 30 minutes and head your way. Will that plan work for you?"

"Sounds good, Don. It's gonna be a long 30 minutes as you can guess, but I can hold on. I'll dig out a candy bar and try to calm my racing heart."

When Phil saw Don coming through the woods toward him he quickly gathered his gear, lowered his bow to the ground with his pull-up string, and descended the tree. The two men smiled huge and exchanged congratulatory knuckles.

"Which direction did he go?" Don asked.

Phil pointed downhill toward a small ravine and answered confidently, "That way. I visually marked the spot where I last saw him. You ready to do some tracking?"

Don grinned big as he watched Phil walk over and jerk the black-colored carbon arrow out of the dirt where it had been stuck. After quickly scanning the arrow from tip to tip, he snapped it into its place in his quiver and started walking in the direction the buck had taken. Don almost had to run to catch up with him.

The two hunters walked about 15 yards and, in the same instant, saw a thumb-sized spill of red liquid on a leaf.

"Yes! Blood!" Phil shouted.

Concerned about Phil's noise level and hoping he would get the hint, Don responded in a whisper, "That is a good sight. Seeing blood drops is the most emotional part of the hunt for me. The sight makes me nearly weak in the knees because I know for sure that I connected."

"Same here. And it's even more intense knowing what size the buck is that I believe I'll find at the end of this trail."

"Amen, Phil. Amen."

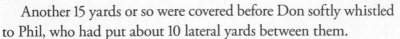

Another 15 yards or so were covered before Don softly whistled to Phil, who had put about 10 lateral yards between them.

Silently mouthing the word "blood," he pointed to the ground.

Phil quickly joined Don to look at a large oak leaf that cradled another splat of crimson. It wasn't quite as big as the first find and contained a little extra coloring that didn't look right. Don carefully picked up the leaf and examined it closely. He handed it to Phil. "Take a look at this. Do you see what I see?"

Though his years as a bow hunter didn't stack up against Don's, Phil had seen enough debris from entrails that he recognized the truth. His shot had been a little further back in the buck's body than he'd thought.

"Can I see that arrow you used, Phil?"

"Sure." Phil got out the arrow and handed it to Don.

Don put the arrow to his nose and whiffed it from tip to tip. The look on his face told Phil the bad news.

"I guess in my rush to get started finding this buck I got a little ahead of myself back there. I should have done the smell test too. I may have a trophy of a lifetime that isn't dead yet, and in fact is probably really sick...sort of like I'm feeling right now."

"Well, let's not jump to conclusions, Phil. He may be more hurt than you think. There's not a heavy amount of stomach content on this arrow, which means you may have barely sliced the front wall of the belly. Let's hope that's the case. Besides, we've got the rest of the day ahead of us. We can take our time and slip along slowly so we don't spook him. We'll look for more blood."

Phil respectfully protested. "Naw. I appreciate your offer, but we both know we can't go on with this search, Don. We gotta back out and let this old boy lie down somewhere and expire. If we go any further we risk pushing him out of the county and out of our hunting area. I hate to admit it, but we...or I...have to come back early afternoon or this evening."

Don wanted to do some more tracking to find more blood and

offer comfort to his partner who was in despair. However, he knew the right decision was to leave the area and return later. "Phil, I have a suggestion."

"What's that, Don?"

"I say we go get some breakfast at my house and call for some help. I've heard you say your dad is really good at finding a wounded deer. Why not ask him to come out with us?"

Unexpected silence followed his idea…and seemed to last forever.

Phil stared toward the area where he last saw the buck. Without saying a word, he stuck his arrow into the ground next to the place where they found the last bloody leaf, turned, and walked in the opposite direction with his head down.

That's how he looked this morning when he left his house, Don noted. He followed his young partner on the 20-minute walk back to the truck and thought about Phil's reaction to his suggestion. Suddenly the pieces of the puzzle started falling into place. *Mentioning his dad triggered the sudden silence.* He walked and thought about it more. Don suspected the argument he'd heard filtering from his neighbor's house that morning was probably not so much about Phil and Marcy and hunting as about Phil and his dad and hunting. With that assumption on his mind, Don trailed Phil out of the woods and prayed for words that might break through the barrier of his young friend's feelings.

The warmth of the cab of the truck felt good as they drove away and headed to the paved road. Phil finally broke his long silence.

"I suppose it would be good to give dad a call and see if he can help us find this deer. He is without a doubt one of the best trackers around. He was always quick to make sure I knew it too."

"I assumed your dad taught you everything he knows about hunting, tracking, and such. Is that right?" Don could see that Phil bristled a little at the question.

"Oh yes sir-eee. He tried to teach me all that stuff, but like everything else he got me into, the harder I tried to do it right, the more I seemed to do it wrong—at least in his opinion. Hunting is the one thing I discovered I really can do, but so far nothing I've killed to this day has ever been big enough for him. The nice 9-point I got three years ago probably weighed in at 190 pounds, and the rack had a good 17- or 18-inch spread on it. What did Dad say about it when I got it back to the house? 'One more point and you'd have yourself a real trophy, Phil.' It was the same when it came to baseball, golf, workin' on cars, and even marrying Marcy. Nothing is ever good enough for that man. I aim to please him, but so far I haven't hit the target."

Don was surprised at Phil's openness, but he appreciated the candor. His confession about the failed attempts to gain his dad's favor revealed the painful fact that the buck they'd left behind today hadn't been the only wounded critter in the woods. And Don knew what he could do to help. As they drove back to town, he quietly worked on his plan.

As they turned onto their street, Don spoke. "Since Marcy is at work, Phil, why don't you come on in to my house. I'll see if I can sweet talk Becky into frying us up some eggs. And you can call your dad from our place and see if he's available."

"Okay," Phil said. But when they pulled up to the curb he announced he would make the call from his house first.

Don gently objected and Phil conceded.

When they entered Don's house, Phil removed his boots at the door and greeted Becky. He went to the phone and called his dad. The conversation lasted only a minute or two.

"Did he say he would help us, Phil?" Don asked when Phil came to the table.

"Yes. He said he'd meet us about a quarter to noon at the barn where we park. He said he'd have no trouble finding the deer."

"Great. Now let's have some chow while we wait."

When Phil pulled up and parked his truck by the barn, his dad was leaning against his vehicle's passenger side door with his arms crossed.

"Howdy, boys."

"Hey, Dad." Phil's voice sounded strained. "This is my neighbor, Don. Don, this is my dad, Frank."

Don extended his hand. "Nice to meet you, Frank. This is one fine son you've got here. And he's quite a hunter too. I saw the brute he arrowed before he got to Phil's stand. Saw him through my binocs. I knew if that critter went by your son there'd be some major adrenalin pumping on the other side of the hill from me. I didn't get an accurate count, but best I can tell he has to be at least a 12-point. And I'm guessing probably well over 200 pounds. I believe I was as nervous as Phil was about the shot, and I'm pumped about finding this deer. Glad you're here to help. Phil tells me you're really good at tracking."

Frank pushed himself away from the truck door with his hands.

"Well, if that buck didn't go down right away, the shot must've been off. Guess we better get to finding it."

Don quietly noted, as did Phil, that no mention was made of the thrill of simply getting the string back on such a mature deer. Frank didn't ask to hear the exciting details about the shot to give his son the opening to share his enthusiasm. No word of encouragement was offered that would help carry the obvious burden of anxiety over a search for a gut-shot deer.

As the trio left the trucks and headed up the hillside toward Phil's tree stand, Don led the charge, Frank was in the middle, and Phil was noticeably well behind. After 300 yards or so Don turned and looked over his shoulder to check on the father and son. Once again he could read Phil's thoughts by the way he walked. His chin was almost resting on his chest as he plodded along. With Frank in the picture, Don wondered whether the heavy worry on his young

friend's shoulders was caused by the dread of not finding the deer…
or the fear of finding it.

As they stood near the tree Phil was in that morning, Don
spoke up. "This is where the deal went down this morning, Frank.
We marked the first find of blood with some toilet paper about 15
yards from here."

The three walked to the spot where the white tissue hung on a
small knee-high sapling. Phil added a little more detail about their
previous search.

"Um…there's another tissue…um…right over there by my
arrow—the one that did the damage."

Frank walked over and pulled the arrow out of the ground. He
looked it over carefully and then put it to his nose. "Yep, there
are digestion juices on this shaft. It's not much though. I have my
doubts about this one."

Don felt the sting of Frank's skepticism and had no doubt that
to Phil it felt like a gunshot to his gut.

As the three of them stood over the second blood spot, Frank
laid out his plan.

"You two spread out about 10 yards on each side of me. We're
going to go down this hill really slow. If someone besides me finds
blood, don't yell out…just softly whistle. I'll come and mark that
spot and then we'll continue. Now, let's take our time and be as
quiet as we can."

Hardly two steps were taken when Phil said, "Stop. I can't believe
it. I forgot my bow. We can't continue this search until I get my
compound! If we find that deer and he's got some life left in him,
I might need to close the deal with another arrow."

Phil's dad cocked his jaw sideways and bit his lower lip. He
didn't have to utter a word to reveal how disgusted he was at his
son's incompetence. He stared into the woods in the direction the
buck had been going.

"I have young legs," Phil asserted. "I can cut the trip in half time-wise. I'll be back in 20 minutes or so. I'm really sorry, guys!"

Don's heart leaped with the opportunity that was suddenly his to claim...if he dared step between Phil and his dad. Don chimed in with some third-party assistance. "We have plenty of daylight left, Phil. We'll wait for you right here."

Like a rabbit leaving its hiding place at the sound of an approaching beagle, Phil bounded off toward his truck. Frank and Don looked anywhere but at each other since they didn't know each other well. Both of them looked through their binoculars, hoping to see a furry body somewhere on the ground.

"How many kids do you have, Frank?" Don finally said, cutting through the silence.

"One boy and one girl. Phil and Deanna. When they were about five and three I thought about having their names changed to Plenty and Quit."

Don chuckled politely, not sure if Frank was being serious or not. "That's a good one, Frank," Don said, choosing to be positive. He waited for a thanks but heard only a proverbial cricket as they continued to endure the long moments of silence.

During the painful lull in their almost wordless wait, Don decided to take a risk. He quietly and quickly coached himself before speaking. *I don't know this man very well. But we're both grown-ups, and whether he can take it or not, I'm going to take the chance and see if I can do something to turn things around for this father and son. I mean, Why not? I should just go for it. I have nothing to lose.*

Feeling amply self-inspired, Don spoke in the friendliest voice he could muster. "Frank, I know we just met, and I only know you through what Phil has told me about you. I've sensed the tension between the two of you. And Phil shared something with me this morning after we abandoned the search that you might want to know. I know I'd want to hear it if I were Phil's father. It wasn't much in terms of information, but his words told me volumes about

something he desperately needs. So I thought you'd want to know about it. Do you want to hear it?"

Frank's expression barely changed, and only a slight compression of his lips and tightening of his jaw muscles revealed he'd heard.

"Do I have a choice?" he finally stated quietly.

"Of course you do," Don responded. "But I think Phil would benefit greatly if you'd hear me out."

"All right. Take your best shot."

"Um…to get straight to the point, Phil needs something from you that he's yet to receive. When we called off the search this morning and got to the truck to head to my place for breakfast, we started talking about how you got him into hunting. In the course of our brief conversation, he opened up about how much he'd like to make you proud of him. To quote him, Phil said, 'nothing ever seems to be good enough for that man. I aim to please him, but so far I haven't hit the target.'"

Frank stared hard at Don and then looked toward the direction of his truck. "That boy knows I love him. I don't know why he would tell you something like that. Seems like he'd come to me with that kind of stuff."

"Well, Frank, I have no doubt Phil knows you love him. But the problem is that he doesn't feel it. Let me explain it this way. My granddad told me one day that he had a 20 dollar bill in his pocket for me. He didn't give it to me right away, and I followed that man everywhere all day long, just waiting for him to let me hold that 20 in my hands. You see, Frank, it was one thing to know that 20 was mine; it was a completely different thing to touch it and feel it. That's a little like Phil right now. He knows you love him, but he needs to feel it. And the way you can touch him with it is with your words, your expressions, and even your body."

"That's a good analogy, Don. The 20 dollar bill description is a good one." Frank looked down at the ground. "I–I g–guess it doesn't take a r–rocket scientist to see there's a bit of a divide b–between Phil

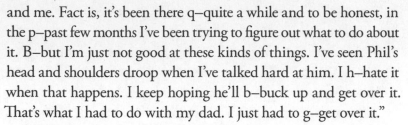

and me. Fact is, it's been there q—quite a while and to be honest, in the p—past few months I've been trying to figure out what to do about it. B—but I'm just not good at these kinds of things. I've seen Phil's head and shoulders droop when I've talked hard at him. I h—hate it when that happens. I keep hoping he'll b—buck up and get over it. That's what I had to do with my dad. I just had to g—get over it."

"Did you get over it, Frank? Or did you just pass your pain on to Phil?"

"Ouch, Don. That hurt. Are you a shrink or something?"

"No, Frank. I'm just like you—a dad who cares about his son."

Frank gathered up a wad of leaves and fresh, moist dirt. He wiped the dried blood off Phil's arrow. "Okay, Don, since you're on a roll, what do you suggest I do about Phil?"

"Well…" Don hesitated. "I guess first you can pray we…"

"I'm not much at prayin', Don," Frank cut in. "You can do that for us."

"We can work on that later if you'd like, Frank. But for now we need to find that buck that's around here somewhere. Hopefully it's dead so it's not suffering anymore. I think the reason Phil has worked so hard at getting a shot at this huge buck we're tracking has everything to do with what we're talking about right now. He's been so consumed by it that I believe it's even affecting his marriage.

"When we do find it, why not grab Phil by the shoulders and give him an 'atta boy' encouragement? Then you can look at me and tell me how amazed and delighted you are that your son could get the string back on such a monster deer. And tell him you want to hear the replay of the details of the hunt, starting from the minute the sun rose this morning.

"And when you do all that, watch his face closely. You'll see a young man who just got the biggest trophy of his life! And it's not the deer, Frank. It's your approval and belief in him. That's what he really wants, Frank. Let him know that when it comes to a father having a son, Phil's the best thing that ever happened to you."

Frank stuck the now very clean arrow back into the ground. After several seconds passed he pursed his lips and then nodded yes.

Within a couple of minutes Phil appeared. "I...(gasp)...told you... (gasp)...I'd be quick. Nineteen minutes!"

"That was pretty quick," Frank replied.

Phil stood upright, smiled at his dad, and then shot a surprised glance at Don.

"No time to waste, Phil. You can catch your breath as we track this beast," Don stated.

It took almost 30 minutes for the three men to cover 200 yards. Frank managed to find several small drops of blood on the way. Each time he did, they regrouped, marked the trail with bright white tissue, and continued on. As they gathered around another find of blood that was half the size of a dime, Frank looked back through the woods and got a visual on the line of escape from the tissue markings. "Looks like he's headed toward the creek, boys. I think it's safe to say there's a reason he's headed toward the water. He must be really hurt. And since we're not but 50 yards from it, Phil, why don't you go on ahead to the creek and take a look around while Don and I follow the trail. And, son, you might want to make sure you step away from the line this deer seems to be following so the blood trail doesn't get ruined."

"Good idea, Dad. I'll be right back." Turning to go, Phil wondered if his ears were playing tricks on him. *Dad actually sounded nice.*

Phil walked 25 yards to the left of the tissue line and headed toward the creek.

Less than a minute later, Don and Frank heard the loud yell of a happy hunter.

"Oh, my word! Here he is. Ya'll get down here!"

Don and Frank dashed to the creek. Don nearly fell into the water as he burst out of the woods and slid to a stop at the creek bank. Frank didn't even stop. Like a schoolboy at a swimming hole, he shot between Phil and Don and landed feet first next to the huge buck.

Standing in the calf-deep stream, Frank excitedly said, "Would you look at this thing? Son, get in here with me and take it in! He's a 12 with a double drop tine. Son!"

Bewildered and elated, Phil looked at Don for a second before frog-leaping into the creek next to his dad. Water splashed over Frank's clothes as he grabbed Phil around the neck with his long arm and said, "Boy, you did it! This one's gotta go on the wall. Wait 'til your mama sees this monster. I can't wait to show my friends pictures of this bruiser."

Phil was speechless.

"Don, can you believe this?" Frank continued. "What nerve it must've taken to get an arrow into this deer. I believe the excitement would've had me messing my britches if it had been me."

Frank slapped his son on his back and added, "I want to hear the tale of this kill—every detail from the time you got up this morning until this moment. Will you share that at suppertime at the house?"

Phil's grin was huge. He reached down and grabbed the massive rack and raised it out of the water.

Don got Frank's attention. When their eyes met, Don drew a circle around his face then pointed to Phil.

Frank nodded and then looked at Phil's face. The sight of his son crying and laughing in the same instant was all he needed to see to know he'd helped his son receive a greater trophy than the one that floated in the creek. As the realization of it washed over him, Frank's eyes watered up and he began to laugh as well.

Don sat on the creek bank and watched a father and son begin a new journey together. As the two of them examined the heavy buck and decided how to get it back to the truck, Don was grateful he was present when a son finally aimed to please and found his dad's heart.

SIX

HUNTING TO LIVE

Chuck's elbows and knees were taking a heavy beating from the rock-hard ground as he crawled through the tall, dry grass on the east Tennessee mountaintop. The clump of small trees he wanted to use as concealment from the eyes of the cow elk he was stalking was still a brutal 40 yards away. Sweat poured off his forehead and blurred his vision, but he wasn't about to take the time to stop and wipe it away. Being too late in getting to the clump where he would most likely get a good shot was not a defeat he was willing to accept.

With his extremities aching and scraped, he slowly rose to his knees and carefully peeked around his leafy blind. He had high hopes that the 10-minute crawl he'd suffered through would yield a shot less than 175 yards with his .30-06. His heart sank. The time-consuming effort had allowed the browsing cow to put 300 yards or so between them again. That shot would require great skill, but Chuck knew he had to take the chance.

Unlike seasons past when taking down a big game animal would have yielded some enjoyable bragging rights with his buddies, pictures with big smiles, and another story to tell grandkids, this hunt was different. Chuck was facing a difficult shot that would determine whether his family of five would have sustaining nourishment in the cold months ahead.

Chuck and many of his friends, as well as a large percentage of citizens, never thought there'd come a time when the cherished line "the land of the free and the home of the brave" would be stripped of one of its core meanings, but it had happened. In the few weeks after the presidential election that had taken place ten years earlier, the changes in the political landscape at first seemed typical to what happens when a new leader takes over at the nation's capital. It was a commonly accepted practice that a new administration would install new cabinet personnel, heads of staff, and appointees in high-caliber positions that would complement the incoming president and his party's agenda.

This time, however, the sweeping changes ushered in a severe shift in attitude and approach to governing. What wasn't expected was how quickly the changes negatively affected the populace as it soon became apparent that the government that was once for the people and by the people had turned into a government over the people.

Though he had campaigned as a moderate, after the oath was taken, the president-elect walked away from the inauguration platform precisely in the direction that he and the willing media had so carefully hidden from the voters during his days on the stump. Shortly after the new president took office, those who had hoped for a change for the better in terms of leadership were confronted with the sobering reality that the commonly accepted liberties that had been treasured in the nation for well over two centuries were suddenly the prime targets of major alterations. The shift to new leadership and the government takeover of banks, car companies, health-care providers, airlines, agricultural industries, and other large businesses became daily news.

Included in the unfortunate swing of the political pendulum was new legislation about gun ownership in the private sector. For people like Chuck, who were wise and prudent users of firearms, the new restrictions established in the name of safety and crime

control represented radical opposition to the spirit and purpose of the Constitution's Second Amendment that had for so long guaranteed that citizens could rightfully possess firearms. To accomplish the goal of banning privately owned guns, heavy taxes were levied on weapon manufacturers. They passed the costs on to store buyers, who in turn drastically raised their prices, which made it difficult for consumers to afford to purchase guns.

And to make it even harder for people, the government instituted long applications forms, a cumbersome verification process, and stiff registering fees before someone could legally acquire a gun. The cost of buying a firearm nearly quadrupled in expense and time and hassle. To further constrict access to firearms, more legislation was passed about making and selling ammunition. Obtaining even the most common calibers of ammo became difficult. All these changes were done under the guise of "citizen safety." And the ruse worked. The citizenry had, for the most part, been successfully disarmed.

When the gun owners got wind of the new governmental restrictions looming on the horizon, they ran en masse to the stores that sold ammo. Within days there was hardly a cartridge or shell to be found anywhere. To many hunters, it was obvious the government hoped to institute regulations to curtail ammo production so the guns already owned would be useless.

Chuck managed to gather a modest stockpile he thought would carry him through two, maybe three, hunting seasons. He figured by being very selective in his shots, he might be able to extend his supply even longer. He hoped the two-term limit on presidential power would mean a return to a more sensible hunting environment within eight years at the most.

What gun owners hadn't counted on was the government pushing through legislation that modified the Twenty-second Amendment and increased the number of terms a sitting president could hold to three. With an uncontested third term looming for the administration, there was little hope the country's situation would improve.

More and more government consolidations of various businesses resulted in extensive job losses. With the disappearing jobs and income came widespread panic fueled by a host of miserable inconveniences. Government-run hospitals began operating on a single-payer system, so long lines of sick people waited for hours to be treated. Unemployment offices had armed guards posted by the doors to monitor and keep in check the angry applicants who had endured long waits in countless lines only to see agents who seemed uncaring and poorly trained.

Funds that could have been raised by drilling and selling oil and other resources were instead collected by frequent hikes in fuel taxes. The result was a nation of frustrated vehicle owners who had to leave their transportation parked in their driveways. And their homes were cold because of the skyrocketing cost of fuel and electricity. But of all the sources of fear and panic the citizens had to deal with, hunger was the most serious one.

People who had never faced any form of public assistance or lack of necessities were facing dire situations. They unraveled emotionally and acted in ways that were destructive and out of character. In cities large concentrations of people got involved in burglary, breaking and entering, and stealing. Former law-abiding citizens were taking food from the shelves of the commodity centers the government set up. Others humbly begged on the street for food or some money so they could buy food. And some resorted to digging through dumpsters for anything edible.

While the multitudes who lived in tightly clustered neighborhoods in the cities were clamoring and fighting daily for their portions of morsels, in the countryside of the rural territories people were also scrambling to feed themselves. They had an advantage: land. Along with sustenance gleaned from gardens and fields, many country folk knew where to find edibles in the wilds, such as blackberries, wild mushrooms, and hickory nuts.

For hunters like Chuck, wild game could provide protein and

more for their families. However, among the community of those who knew how to track down an animal, kill it, and prepare it for consumption there was serious concern because the legal right to hunt that had already been reduced drastically was still being attacked.

The restricted hunting that had come about under the names of safety and animal rights, along with the shortage of ammo, resulted in an unexpected threat to the government-operated crop farms. Deer herds, flocks of turkeys, elk herds, and other animals that had been carefully nurtured and managed by hunters after nearly becoming extinct were reaching alarming numbers. The natural browsing areas couldn't support the population, so the hungry droves of wildlife devastated stands of corn, soy beans, and other produce.

Farm operators desperately needed the assistance of hunters to control the ravenous animals, but radical environmental groups held too much influence in the government and successfully stopped any animal control efforts. Worse, they also used their influence to seriously curtail the issuing of hunting licenses and tags. To further discourage hunting and inflame the nonhunters against the hunters, the environmental groups managed to change the familiar "hunting license" to "kill animals permit."

Though it seemed not much could be done about the situation, most hunters agreed that what was missing in the minds of the government-appointed controllers of natural resources was rational thinking. The "wildlife managers" refused to admit hunters served a useful purpose and could provide food for quite a few people through selective culling of the roaming herds and flocks. And with fewer animals, the loss of crops would be significantly reduced—a win–win for everyone.

But the vicious bickering of opposing views created a tornado of arguments among the left and right. The result was that hunters like Chuck were facing the possibility that the elk permits they'd applied for and were granted through a lottery system might never be available again.

As he rested his .30-06 on a limb of one of the scrub trees he was using for cover, Chuck found the cow in his scope. He'd never hunted elk before. They'd been reintroduced into Tennessee, but he'd always hunted deer. And now here he was, and a lot was riding on this shot. The image of the hungry faces of his children and wife filled his mind. And the pressure of getting food on this, the last day of hunting season, and the fact that it was possibly the last afternoon of the last legal season for hunting in the nation tampered with his confidence.

To combat the unwelcome anxiety, Chuck took a deep breath and exhaled slowly. Looking through the scope he noticed the cow had stopped and was grazing in one spot. Hoping she wouldn't decide to move on immediately, he watched her closely as he quickly dug his range finder out of its belt holster and measured the distance: 331 yards.

With the crosshairs raised to the top of the cow's shoulder, Chuck looked away from his scope for a few seconds to observe the tops of the grass in the field in front of him for wind speed and direction. His best guess was a 15-mile-an-hour wind coming left to right. With that information, he replaced the crosshairs on the elk's back but then slightly moved the rifle left and placed the crosshairs just above the forward section of the paunch. He took another deep breath and gradually exhaled. As he slowly pressed on the trigger he whispered, "Lord, please bless this bullet!"

His short-but-earnest prayer was answered. The cow stumbled with the impact of the bullet and then ran away from Chuck's position. Though he was sure he had connected with the elk, the normal elation that accompanies a well-placed shot wasn't present. The report of the .30-06 seemed to echo forever across the mountaintop and probably down to the valley.

Chuck had heard about "backwoods bandits" who used force to steal the game hunters downed. They would take the unregistered meat and sell it to dealers, who would then resell it at enormous

profit to cash-hungry city-based buyers. Though he wasn't totally sure they were active in this area, he didn't want to hang around to find out if the sound of his shot had stirred up their hornet's nest. There would be no afterglow of the kill and no jubilant phone calls. What awaited him instead was the need to quickly gather his equipment, hurry to find the cow that he was sure would soon expire, and claim ownership of the valuable carcass.

With that reality electrifying his mind and heart like a cattle prod, Chuck hustled back to the spot where he'd shed his backpack a few minutes earlier to make stalking easier. When he got to his gear he looked back toward the tree where he'd taken the shot. For a fleeting second he felt a familiar rush of satisfaction about the stalk and the lengthy shot and was tempted to take a minute and revel in it. But he quickly suppressed the joy and forced his tired and beat-up legs to turn toward the spot he had visually marked as the last place he'd seen the elk.

Chuck headed across the field, and it felt like it took a full century to get to where the cow had been standing when he pulled the trigger. With his rifle ready for a quick finishing shot if necessary and his thumb resting on the safety, he slowly zigzagged the escape route area the elk had taken. He found a sizable splotch of blood on the ground. Soon following more easily seen pools of blood, he walked toward a stand of tall timber below the ridgeline. He was sure the elk was mortally wounded. After another 20 steps and now standing just inside the shadowy woods, he saw the large body of the cow lying 50 yards ahead of him. As he approached the animal, he couldn't help observing out loud its enormous size. "Wow! I knew they were big, but this is huge! What am I going to do with this elk? I've never field dressed something that rivals the size of a horse. Yikes. Lord, I'm going to need Your help here!"

Though the pre-noon weather in the higher elevations was cool that day, Chuck hoped the temperature would drop even more as the afternoon wore on. The colder it was, the better it was for the

meat he'd labored so hard to find and kill. He hurried with the field dressing preparations. He'd never worked on such a large animal, so he would be applying knowledge he'd mainly garnered from books, pictures, and conversations.

Before he began the huge task of carving the elk and shuttling it to his truck, Chuck decided to send a text message to his wife regarding his success and that his return home would be delayed. Knowing technology existed that could intercept his message, he carefully entered, "Great hike today. Last two miles will be a chore."

Mary Beth smiled big when she read the text message in the window of her phone. She'd hoped and prayed for his success. The code words were all there just like they had rehearsed. "Great hike" meant his hunt had been safe and successful. "The last couple of miles are going to be a chore" was code for "the animal is heavy, and I'm going to be late getting home because it's going to take me a while to get it off the mountain."

Within a minute or so Chuck's text tone alerted him that there was a message on his phone. He flipped it open and read, "Glad you had a good walk. See you later."

Chuck put his phone back in his pocket and gazed at the 400 pounds of fresh elk that lay at his feet. After a minute or so of absorbing the reality of it, he knelt down and patted the animal's large belly. As he mentally went over what one of his hunting books had said about how to begin the process, a voice from behind him broke the silence and gave his heart a jolt.

"You have no clue where to start, do you?"

Chuck stood and swung around, rifle semi-raised. Before him stood a tall, thin figure with a crossbow hanging by a sling off his shoulder. A small gear bag was attached to the empty pack frame on his back. Though he looked imposing at first, Chuck caught a glimpse of the calming smile that occupied the stranger's face.

"You startled me. I can't believe I didn't hear you walk up!"

The stranger removed his cap and wiped his brow. "From the way you've been shaking your head while gawking at that brown furred mountain at your feet, it appears your mind may have been way too muddled to hear anything. It's either that or you can't type into your phone and listen at the same time. Am I right on one of those?"

Still unable to fully appreciate the presence of anyone at the scene who wasn't family, Chuck laughed nervously and responded, "I guess you're right on both counts. Care to tell me your name?"

They both knew that in the times they lived in people were less willing to trust anyone but close acquaintances. If the hiker shared his identity, he was probably safe and not out to kill Chuck and steal the meat.

"My name is Keith. I live at the base of this mountain—on the east side. My place is right at the edge of this national forest. I've hunted this area all my life, and I know it like the back of my 58-year-old hand. I've had my share of experience with these elk since the Forest Service reintroduced them into our territory several years ago. And I'll tell you this, finding you was not a chore at all. That .06 of yours has quite a set of lungs. I wasn't too far from you when you fired. From where I was above you, I could see you through my binoculars. I watched your entire stalk. You did really good except for one thing."

Chuck felt a little exposed. "And what did I do wrong?"

"You came up here alone, my friend. Surely you knew how large these animals can be and how difficult it can be to field dress a beast like this by yourself. And with the meat war going on, I sure hope you knew how vulnerable a lone hunter can be."

Chuck lowered his head a bit. "You're partially right. I've seen these elk from a distance, but it wasn't until I got close to this cow that I really understood how massive they can be. That's when I realized that field dressing it was going to be quite a job.

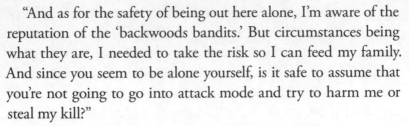

"And as for the safety of being out here alone, I'm aware of the reputation of the 'backwoods bandits.' But circumstances being what they are, I needed to take the risk so I can feed my family. And since you seem to be alone yourself, is it safe to assume that you're not going to go into attack mode and try to harm me or steal my kill?"

"You assume correctly. I didn't catch your name."

"My name is Charles, but family and friends call me Chuck. I'm glad to meet you, Keith."

"Chuck, not many folks I know are hunting with rifles these days. They make too much noise, and noise can attract trouble. The quiet nature of archery cuts down on the possibility of tangling with the creeps who think they can help themselves to any animal in these parts. When necessary, the hunters I know sneak in, kill quickly with an almost silent weapon, and then quietly take it home. Do you have a bow or a crossbow?"

"Archery is something I never did get into. Most of the people I knew growing up used guns, so I haven't used a bow much at all. You're right about it being safer. It's too bad I never learned."

Keith removed his bow from his shoulder and leaned it against a tree. "While you were finding ammo for that loudspeaker of yours, I was buying every arrow I could find that fits my draw length on my compound. I also bought every bolt I could find for this beauty." Keith patted the stock of his recurve crossbow. "One nice thing about an arrow—you can use it again if you find it after a shot and it's undamaged. Those shaftless arrows you shoot are gone for good. And since bows are harder to conceal and use in close quarters, as when committing crimes, the folks who are messin' with our right to bear arms think nothing of these weapons. They probably don't know how good some of us are with these stringed toys."

"Maybe so," Chuck agreed. "But the shot I got today wouldn't have been one that a stick thrower could have taken."

Keith nodded in agreement but countered the thought. "You

have a point, but don't forget that if I heard your .30-06 announce your success, so did a dozen other hungry hunters—not to mention some guys who are probably waiting for you to load this critter up and haul it off the mountain for them. Fact is, you would have done well to fire another four or five rounds after your first shot hit the mark. The way I figure it, a series of shots tells the bad guys you don't know what you're doing so you're probably not successful and they shouldn't waste their time with you."

"That makes sense, I guess. But I don't have the ammo to spare for that kind of trickery."

Keith unbuttoned his sleeves and rolled the material up toward his elbow. "Well, if you stick with using a rifle, and if there is a next time, now you know. Right now you could obviously use some help getting this beast ready to sneak past those lazy, worthless meat grabbers hiding down below. If you want the help, I'm your man."

"My mama didn't raise no fool, friend. If you've tackled one of these overgrown girls before, please show me the way. Tell me what to do. I'm all ears."

For the next hour Keith put on a butchering clinic as he skillfully cut, sliced, and sawed on the heavy cow. Chuck's job was simple. He pulled on legs, yanked on hide and tossed unusable entrails and other unwanted body parts aside. As the two men worked together they found an easy camaraderie. They shared how they learned to love the hunt and their fear of losing the freedoms their fathers and grandfathers had fought and even died for. The time passed quickly, and a friendship blossomed in the way that happens when two individuals discover they share common ground.

"Keith, do you have children?"

"Got two who are grown and married."

"Boys, girls, both? And where do they live?"

Keith straightened up and removed his bloody latex gloves. He stuffed them in a ziplock bag as he answered, "One boy, one girl. They both live about five miles from us. One north and one south of us. They each have two young'uns. My wife and I love those grandkids. Three boys and one girl so far. It's really hard to see them struggle through these times our nation is in.

"My son is barely making ends meet with all the taxes on everything he earns. My son-in-law isn't doing much better, even though he's well schooled like my son is. The girls have given up so much of their lives to keep the homes afloat. They do the best they can, but still it's a hard row to hoe for both little families. Truth is, I hate the downturn of our nation more for them than I do for me. They don't know the America you and I grew up in, and it hurts deep to face the sad possibility they may never know it."

Chuck nodded.

"You're one blessed man to have gotten a permit to nail this big old girl. The effort you put into this kill was impressive to watch. I commend you for it. Now, let's quit jawing and hang a front and a rear quarter high in a tree so we can take the first load of these future steaks to your vehicle."

Chuck thanked his willing helper and finished wrapping one of the front quarters and two long and lean tenderloins together in a game bag. He piled the heavy load onto his right shoulder and grunted. "Whoa, Nellie! I've killed whitetails that didn't come close to weighing this much."

Keith finished tying a rear quarter to his pack frame and, as he lifted it onto his back, added with a bear-like growl, "And this hunk of flesh feels like it might be pushing at least 65 pounds. Even though our knees are going to get the brunt of the descent work, I'm glad it's downhill! Are you ready? Don't forget to grab your weapon... just in case we need to protect your kill."

Keith's face was red with strain as he looked up toward the sky and assessed the weather conditions. "I believe the temps are low enough that the quarters we'll have to come back for won't spoil. You can thank God for that blessing."

"Amen, brother!"

Loaded like a pair of mules, the two friends headed downhill, making sure every step was deliberate and sure. Every 50 yards or so Keith stopped and tied a short strip of plastic orange ribbon to low-hanging branches as trail markers.

"These orange ribbons will lead back up to your other two quarters. They'll be there for you in case something happens to make us split up. I'm not saying it will…I'm just being cautious. I'd sure hate for you to not reap the full benefit of your hunt today."

Chuck said thanks for the ribbon trail and Keith added, "By the way, when we get to the bottom of this mountainside I suggest we not go straight to your truck. You left it at the Thomas Creek parking area, right?"

"Right. I didn't have a lot of choice."

"That's precisely why meat thugs love to watch that place. I'm thinking we should drop off the hill about a quarter of a mile up the hard road from that parking lot. We can stash the quarters just off the pavement. Then we'll pick up the second load and take them down. After that you can loop around and go to your truck. That way anyone who is watching will think you came up empty handed. They'll leave you alone, and you can take off, pick up your stash, and head home. You can check it in with the Tennessee Wildlife Resources Agency online. How's that for a good plan?"

"Sounds good, Keith. I sure appreciate all you're doing for me. I couldn't have gotten this much done by myself."

Keith tore off another few inches of ribbon. "No problem. I'm shooting for the good feeling award. Not much of that goes on anymore, so when I get a chance I go for it."

With 80 minutes of good daylight left and barely enough energy to spare, the two hunters delivered one load to the roadside and completed the hard climb back to the tree holding the remaining two quarters. Keith wiped the sweat off his forehead with his sleeve and admitted, "Between that hunk of elk flesh that pushed me down the hill and that climb back up here, I could sure use some rest. But we'd better not do that. How are you doing, Chuck?"

Chuck swallowed water from the bottle he'd taken from his pack. "I have one more trip in me, and that's about it. My legs are thankful it's downhill all the way too. My poor knees are not going to be happy about any of this tomorrow, but I'll make it today."

Keith pulled the meat out of the tree and loaded his pack and helped Chuck load his. Just as Keith was about to hoist the pack frame onto his shoulder Chuck stopped him.

"Hold on, Keith. Before you do that, tell me something. Where do you live from here?"

Keith pointed across the field toward the scrub trees Chuck had used for cover. "If you go to the left of that clump of trees where you took your shot today, and then go over the ridge and straight down, my house is at the bottom of the mountain. It's about an hour and a half walk from here. I could make that walk blindfolded."

"Are there any roads to cross on the way to your place?"

Keith looked toward the field. "Nope. Not a one. It's all woods and a few open fields."

Chuck tucked his shirt into his pants and adjusted his belt in preparation for hoisting a quarter onto his shoulder. "My friend, it has been an extreme pleasure to have met you today. I've been meaning to check to see if there might be wings on your back underneath that pack frame because your help has been nothing less than divine. Surely you're an angel God sent to help me."

Keith smiled. "Nope, I'm just a man like you."

"Now I want to do something for you. Wrestle that rear quarter onto your shoulders and take it home. Feed those little grand-munch-kins. You've certainly earned it with all the help you've given me. I'm guessin' it will yield nearly as much good meat as the whitetail you gave up hunting today to help me. How does that sound?"

"This meat is better than pure gold. Are you sure? What would possess you to do such a thing?"

Chuck grinned. "In the words of a good friend, 'I guess I'm shooting for the good feeling award 'cause not much of that goes on anymore.' And I can find my way to the road easily with that good ribbon trail to follow."

The two men adjusted their packs and then shook hands vigorously.

"Not too many years ago there was a bumper sticker that a lot of hunters put on their vehicles," Chuck said. "I had one on my truck. Maybe you remember it. It said, 'I live to hunt.'"

"Yes." Keith smiled. "I remember it. If I'd had one I would've put it on my Jeep."

Chuck used one hand to balance the front quarter and the other to drape his rifle sling on his shoulder. "Well, I guess for guys like you and me the days of living to hunt are a thing of the past. From now on it looks like we'll be hunting to live."

Keith picked up his crossbow. "Amen, my brother."

"It was great meeting you, Keith."

"You too, Chuck. Perhaps we'll meet on the mountain again."

They shook hands one more time and then headed out.

SEVEN

FRESHEN THE SCRAPE

The first-period bell sounded on the opening day of the new year at Keller High School. Eric quickly crammed some yet-to-be-used books into his locker and then turned to join the swarm of students that filled the hall as they hurried to classrooms. When he merged into the flood of bodies walking in the direction he needed to go, he fell in behind two girls. They were talking so loudly he could hear their conversation clearly.

The girl on the right asked a question, and when the girl on the left responded, her answer made Eric hear the sound of angels singing. Actually, it was the singing of just one little cherub—the one with a small arrow and bow and tiny red hearts floating around his head like a halo. Little Cupid's arrow had found its mark. Eric had fallen in love, but the girl who was talking wasn't aware of his tumble.

"I appreciate you asking me to try out for cheerleading, but I can't do it. If I did, I'd have to miss most of bow season."

Eric picked up his pace a little to close the small gap between the she-hunter and him. He turned his head slightly to better hear the rest of her statement.

"Dad's got some alfalfa planted on this one field, and it's going to be a deer hotspot. I can't miss it. I hope our team wins, but they'll have to do it without me to cheer them on. I'll be in the woods."

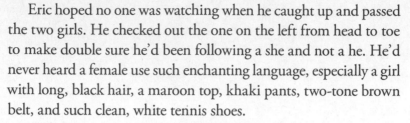

Eric hoped no one was watching when he caught up and passed the two girls. He checked out the one on the left from head to toe to make double sure he'd been following a she and not a he. He'd never heard a female use such enchanting language, especially a girl with long, black hair, a maroon top, khaki pants, two-tone brown belt, and such clean, white tennis shoes.

As the trio neared the chemistry lab where Eric would have to exit, his heart pounded. The two girls split off, and the young huntress turned left into the same door he needed to enter.

"Thank you, God!" Eric whispered—but not as softly as he'd intended.

The girl wheeled around on her heels, looked at Eric, smiled, and said, "For what?"

Stunned and embarrassed, Eric answered, "Uh…what…uh, for what?"

"What are you thanking God for?"

Cornered by his little prayer that wasn't intended to be overheard by earthly ears, Eric quickly tried to think of an answer that wouldn't leave him looking like a complete bungling fool in the eyes of his new interest. He decided the best policy was honesty.

"Well, as I followed you and your friend down the hall, I couldn't help but overhear your answer to her about not trying out for cheerleading because it would interfere with bow season. I had no idea that a girl would like that sort of thing—especially a pretty girl like you."

Eric instantly regretted the "pretty girl" part. He hadn't planned on that coming out. He went silent and to avoid the awkwardness of his slip he acted like he was losing his grip on his books. As he faked fumbling with the load in his arm he silently prayed the girl would offer some sort of response. He was afraid it would be rejection, but her reply made his heart soar.

"Are you a hunter?"

Eric could tell by the extended, high-pitched prolonged sound of

the "r" at the end of the last word of her question that her inquiry included not only a request for a yes or no but also his name.

"I do love to hunt, and my name is Eric. What's yours?"

"I'm Lisa. Do you shoot a bow?"

Eric couldn't believe he'd just heard three of his most favorite concepts in one short answer: a pretty girl's name, shooting, and bow. He was forming his next words when the teacher spoke up and directed the class members to take their seats.

Pulled out of the clouds and back to the terrestrial reality of crucibles, Bunsen-burners, and hard-to-understand words, Eric looked at Lisa, smiled politely, and reached into his shirt pocket for a picture he'd brought to school to show his best friend and hunting buddy, Joseph. In one smooth motion he flashed the photo in front of Lisa's face and replaced it into his pocket. Her eyes widened when she got a glimpse of it. She looked at Eric and smiled widely. With a quick swing of her head from left to right she flipped her hair out of her eyes, nodded approvingly, and said, "Nice. I want to hear more."

They both found empty seats in the room, and class got underway. Eric was sure his heart was going to melt into the ankle-high hiking boots he was wearing. He hardly heard a word the teacher said because he was too busy watching the clock hands go around in anticipation of the hour-ending bell that would reunite him with her.

Finally the bell rang and Eric gathered his books and watched Lisa prepare to leave. He had to do a little extra shuffling of papers to time it just right so he was at the door the same moment she reached it. He did the gentlemanly thing and gave her the "please go first" hand motion.

"Thank you, Eric. May I see that picture again?"

Eric's hand dove into his shirt pocket and retrieved the glossy paper he never dreamed could be used as a "babe magnet." He passed it to Lisa as he explained, "I took that shot out of a tree stand on my uncle's farm with my camera about a month ago. As you can

see, the buck is still in velvet. Not long after that I saw him again, and he had it all rubbed off."

Lisa studied the photo for a few seconds. "He's at least a 10, nice G-2's, and looky there! He's got a drop tine. We didn't get to see many deer like that where we used to live. I bet he's pushing 190 pounds and might score in the low 140s easy."

Eric's heart rate went off the chart.

As she handed the picture back to Eric, she asked, "Got some stands up on that guy's routes? You know if you don't get him during the first few days of season, he'll go totally nocturnal on you. You won't see him again until velvet time next year...unless he decides to make a target of himself during rut."

Eric couldn't take it anymore and the words "Will you marry me?" formed on his tongue. He caught himself just in time and opted for saying something less risky. "What's the possibility of getting together later and making sure our bows are shooting right for opening day of deer season? We only have three weeks to go."

Lisa looked down the hall at the clock that hung from the ceiling. "I have 45 seconds to get to the gym, so I don't have time to give you my phone number, but the answer to your question is yes, we should do some shooting together. I'd like that."

Eric held the picture of the deer in one hand and quickly reached into his shirt pocket and pulled out another piece of paper he'd written on during class. He handed it to Lisa. "Here's my phone number...well, it's my folks' phone number. Call me this evening, and we'll figure out where to do some shooting."

Lisa took the piece of paper and held it in her hand as she waved and hurried off. Eric stood motionless and waited for the dream to end. He heard none of the clamoring of hurrying seniors and juniors. He didn't hear the voice of his best friend, Joseph, until he felt a hard punch on his right arm.

"Eric! Time to go, Eric. You have 15 seconds to get to second period."

Roused from a deep trance, Eric felt Joseph's finger poking him on his temple. He slapped his friend's hand away and shook his head. "Man, did you see that girl? Did you hear the way she talked? Have I died and gone to heaven?"

15 years later

The memory of those questions he'd asked Joseph in the hallway of Keller so many years ago, along with all the things Lisa had said, echoed through Eric's mind. He looked through the woods from his tree stand. The morning had been unfruitful in terms of sightings, but the briskness of the third Saturday of the October archery season was plenty of reward for a soul-weary hunter.

Eric's exhaustion wasn't the result of what had happened in previous years. Always before his tiredness at this time of year had centered on the "up every day before dawn" pursuit of whitetail. He wished that's what had him worn ragged this year. His heart was heavy because of something he still couldn't wrap his mind around.

As it turned out, the two girls Eric followed down the hall on that first day of school 15 years earlier were new students at Keller due to the consolidation of three county schools. Lisa, who had indeed accepted Eric's invitation on that opening day of school to do some shooting with their compound bows, became the love of his life—and eventually his bride. Through Eric, Lisa's friend Karly was introduced to Joseph. Try as she might, she couldn't escape the charm of Joseph's nearly emerald-green eyes. They tied the knot when they were 21 years young, just a few weeks after Eric and Lisa's big event took place.

As Eric sat in his climber and recalled some of the details of the life journey the four friends had been on, he quietly chuckled at how wonderful his relationship with Lisa was. During their junior and senior years of high school, their mutual interest in archery and hunting created a unique love connection, one that was admired and even envied by many of their classmates—especially the guys. Eric quickly figured out that the way to Lisa's heart was through her tree stand. Gladly he made every effort he could think of to capture and keep her blaze-orange affection. He learned that for Lisa a good date was when he took her to events such as outdoor expos and whitetail seminars.

The unusual nature of their relationship continued through their dating after high school. One particularly fun evening out that Lisa enjoyed was attending a wild game dinner at their church. They went together, both of them decked out in clean and pressed camo gear. Looking much finer than any couple in Mossy Oak should be permitted to, they took their places at their designated table. Eric smiled as he recalled how much Lisa talked about the part of the event when they held hands tightly as the door prizes were being handed out, quietly praying they'd win the grand prize. They had romantically filled out only one card for the drawing, highlighting their couple status. They couldn't believe it when their names were called! Giddily holding hands, they went forward to claim the .308 Weatherby rifle.

After high school graduation, which they both attended while mischievously wearing camo gloves and heavy rubber boots that didn't match their gold gowns, they both commuted from their homes to a small college in a nearby town that was conveniently close to their favorite woods. Though they both did well at college, they tried hard not to let academics interfere too much with archery season and their dating schedule. After three years of college and commencement, they took jobs in their hometown. At the ripe age of 21, they tied the knot.

As Eric looked for signs of deer life around his stand, his thoughts drifted to Joseph. His best friend was hunting with him. Joseph was located at a field-edge ladder stand about 1000 yards down the creek. He thought of what a big hunting fan Joseph was, but then

he'd met Karly and pulled back. He didn't seem to struggle with her lack of interest in what had been his passionate hobby. That she didn't embrace the camo crowd simply didn't matter to him. As far as he was concerned, her long and curly blond hair, her deep-blue eyes, and her coo-like-a-dove voice was all the doe a young buck could ever wish for. Convinced she was worth any sacrifice, he'd become so intent on winning Karly's heart that he'd gone to legendary lengths to impress her. His exploits were still talked about in the halls of Keller High School.

Perhaps the most talked about escapade in Joseph's wild efforts to win Karly's love involved four king-sized cotton bed sheets. He sewed the white sheets together, spray painted a few words on the huge banner, and snuck in late at night to hang the massive sign over the main entrance of the school, which just happened to face the highway. The next morning when Karly's parents turned the corner in their car to enter the school property to drop her off, everyone in the car nearly fainted when they saw the cotton expanse: Karly, I ♥ you! Prom? With me?

Eric smiled at the thought of what Karly and her family—especially Karly's dad—must have thought when they saw Joseph's homemade banner. Though it had shocked everyone, apparently Joseph had reached Karly's heart because they attended the prom together. In the eyes of their classmates who had gathered at the front of the building to gawk at the humongous bed-sheet sign, the two of them seemed custom made for each other. Eric and Lisa thought so as well.

But now Joseph and Karly were a long way from being a happy couple. Somewhere on the trail of love they'd walked for 15 years, something had gone wrong. Eric shifted his weight on his tree stand seat to seek some relief for his derriere. As he continued to scan the woods, he contemplated Joseph's phone call a few days earlier. Eric knew his friend well enough to hear the discouragement in his voice as he shared how he and Karly had drifted apart over the last half-dozen years. Joseph struggled to verbalize his state of mind. He dug deep for courage and then spilled his emotional guts to Eric. Joseph's words had felt like a dagger in his heart.

"As a husband, I feel like I'm just wandering around in a marital wilderness. The uncertainty is really scary and unsettling. Karly and I used to be so close, but now we're not. Have you and Lisa noticed the change?"

"Yes, we talked about it a few weeks ago. Body language can reveal a lot more than words. I've sensed a coldness between the two of you more than once. At first we thought the two of you were in a spat or maybe Karly was going through a hard time…you know… that monthly thing women go through. Then Lisa noticed that Karly being critical and unhappy seemed to be a regular thing. I'm a little dense so I didn't notice it as soon as she did, but after she pointed it out I started watching. The discord is visible."

"What do you think I can do to get Karly back on my side, Eric?"

As the late October sun filtered through the trees and warmed Eric's chilled body, he felt the regret of not being skilled enough in counseling to immediately offer suggestions to help his friend. The best he could do was "Let me think about it, and I'll get back to you." And then he added what any hunter would say in a moment of such raw honesty. "Let's go hunting early next week." While some friends might resent such an answer, Joseph heard what Eric really meant: "Let's go hunting and we'll talk about it some more."

The morning was wearing on as the two friends hunted. Knowing they were less than an hour from packing it in and heading to their favorite burger joint, Eric continued to work on something encouraging to say to Joseph.

Suddenly he saw movement about 50 yards in front of his stand. He peered intently through the multicolored leaves. A buck! His hand tightened around the handle of his riser, and he immediately stood up to prepare for a shot.

When the buck, a nice eight point, had covered another 20 yards, Eric's emotions leveled off. The deer stopped beneath a licking branch and began a ritual that was a show to behold. Eric quietly watched as the heavy deer intermittently tongued and nosed the tips of the branch. Then he swiped the base of his antlers on it. After a minute or so of that odd behavior, he gouged at the bark and dirt with his front hooves, deepening the scrape he'd made beneath the branch. Then the buck carefully positioned himself and urinated on the freshly upturned dirt and scraped bark. Though both strange and normal, Eric knew that what he had just seen was a practice solely meant to attract his female friends in the area.

Suddenly he knew what advice to give to Joseph! As he rehearsed the thoughts he would share, the buck wandered off to Eric's right and followed one of the creek trails. Eric quickly dug for his radio and buzzed Joseph.

"Hey, man, a nice eight-point just worked a scrape about 30 yards from me and then headed your way. Be watching, Joseph. You might get a chance at him in a little while."

"Thanks for the heads up. I'll let you know if something monstrous my way comes."

Eric waited about 20 minutes and was just about to succumb to the temptation to buzz Joseph again when his radio announced a call coming in. "Yea, man. What's happening?"

"I just stuck a buck, and I think it's the one you saw! After I arrowed him he ran by me, and I bet he didn't go 49 yards before piling up. I'm looking at him right now. I almost blew it. He's got another scrape just a few yards from me, and I didn't know it this morning, but I must've stepped right in the middle of it when I walked in. When he put his nose to it he got really nervous. I thought he was going to hightail it out of here. But he stood there trying to decide what to do and that gave me time to get to full draw. My 20-yard pin was right on the money. I can't believe it!"

Eric pumped his arm in victory. He pushed the radio button to

respond. "Way to go, Joseph! Nothing—and I mean nothing—brightens the day like making a great shot. I'll dismount and head your way. I should be there in 10 minutes or so. I expect you to have that deer gutted and ready for dragging by the time I get there." Eric chuckled.

Joseph laughed. "Well, old buddy, I've got some bad news for you. I left my knife in the truck. I hope you have yours!"

"No problem, friend. You can use my knife, and I'll watch you work while I eat my Fifth Avenue and have some coffee. And while you're carvin' we'll do a little talkin'. I think I've come up with something that might help you and Karly."

Within 15 minutes Joseph heard some noise in the brush. He looked up to see Eric walking toward him.

"What a beast!" Eric commented as he walked around Joseph's kill. After setting his gear down, Eric said, "We might as well get started."

Working in silence, Joseph and Eric manhandled the heavy carcass into a position to field dress.

Breathing hard, Eric said, "Okay, it's all yours. Here's my field dressing kit. It's got everything you need—skinning knife, hand saw, gloves—the works. You work; I'll have some coffee."

Joseph accepted the kit, opened it, and pulled out the knife. "Works for me," he said, turning to the deer. He carefully made an incision in the buck's lower belly. He turned the razor-sharp blade of the knife upward and placed it just inside the short incision in the hide at the buck's lower belly. Then he carefully placed his index and middle finger on each side of the blade to guide it as he cut toward the deer's ribs.

After a little while Eric asked, "Are you ready to hear what I've come up with that might help you and Karly?"

"I'm all ears."

"This morning I watched this buck freshen a scrape and mess

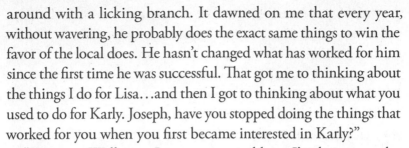

around with a licking branch. It dawned on me that every year, without wavering, he probably does the exact same things to win the favor of the local does. He hasn't changed what has worked for him since the first time he was successful. That got me to thinking about the things I do for Lisa…and then I got to thinking about what you used to do for Karly. Joseph, have you stopped doing the things that worked for you when you first became interested in Karly?"

"Hmmm. Well, yes, I guess you could say I've let up on the romance stuff. Between the demands of two kids, running a construction business, and everything else that consumes my time, I haven't had the time or energy. Maybe I have slacked off too much when it comes to Karly."

Eric nodded his head and waited to see if Joseph would continue.

"So, Eric, what you are suggesting is that I freshen the scrape?"

"You got it. Go back and do those things you used to do that made Karly's eyes light up and her heart palpitate. Do you know the 'Three R's' of a good marriage?"

Joseph took the bait. "Nope, but I have a feeling I'm going to. Go ahead. Give it to me straight."

"In the book of Revelation, second chapter, there's a message to the church at Ephesus. The believers in that town had left their first love for Christ. They'd lost their fervor, their enthusiasm, their dedication. To get back their 'first love' they were told to do three things."

Eric touched his right index finger to the fingers on his left hand as he spoke. "One, 'remember therefore from where you have fallen.' In other words, think about and recall the joy of where you used to be with Karly. Two, 'repent.' Tell God you're sorry for slacking off with Karly. And three, 'Re-do.' That's my personal paraphrase of what the Ephesus church was told to do. That is, 'do the first works'—what you did when you were on fire for Karly."

Joseph stood and stretched, arching his back. "Wow! That's in the Bible? That's good stuff. I feel some hope coming on."

Eric continued. "Don't forget, dude. You set a high standard for yourself back in high school. Remember that basketball court-sized bed-sheet sign you made for her before the prom? That's going to be a hard act to follow, but you sure made an impression on Karly that day. And remember the 'Joseph plus Karly' crop circle thing you did in the cornfield? I thought you'd go to jail for that one. You're lucky that farmer let you work off the cost of the damaged corn. Working the hay wagon or going to jail...the choice was pretty clear, wasn't it? You sure did some shenanigans back then, but they must have done the trick because Karly fell in love with you."

Joseph laughed and added, "I would rather have gone to jail. I hoisted more than 1500 bales of hay for that farmer. That's almost capital punishment. But it sure was sweet to see our names in that cornfield on the evening news when they showed the aerial view. Karly was proud of that one."

Eric grinned at how Joseph managed to still brag about being on TV. "Well, Mr. Do It Big, I think you've done the remembering part of the Three R's. Now it's time to do some repenting, and then you've gotta think of something dramatic to get Karly's attention. And it has to be something significant."

Joseph opened his folding handsaw and prepared to saw through the buck's sternum. "I think you're right about this idea, Eric. It never occurred to me that I made myself a hard act to follow. Now that I think about it, all these years you've kept doing for Lisa what you've done from the beginning. You're a blessed man to have a woman who is so excited about hunting. She'd track you down and tag you if you spent money on roses instead of arrows."

Eric thought about the days when he was dating Lisa. His high school friends used to make fun of the "romantic" gifts he'd buy for Lisa—arrows, targets, and other gear. He told them more than once that it wasn't that she didn't like flowers, which he did give her from time to time, but she knew dollars spent on broadheads,

hand warmers, and black powder for her .50 caliber muzzleloader meant spending time together outdoors.

"I guess I've conditioned Karly to expect more—especially more than nothing, which is what's been happening," Joseph continued. "I'm not sure where and when I started forgetting the rule of offering signs of how much I love her. I guess it didn't happen overnight. But maybe I can shock her back into believing in me again by telling her—and showing her—how much she still means to me. I'll think of something. This could be fun!"

Eric recognized the look in Joseph's eyes. It indicated that his wheels of imagination were turning. "I can't wait to see what you're gonna come up with—I think. I hope I'm around to see whatever you plan!"

"Well, whatever it is, it's gotta be a major freshening of the scrape! Okay, I'm finished here. Are you ready to drag this deer to the truck? If you'll pull the hardest, you can come over tomorrow afternoon. I'll grill the back straps just for you. I appreciate you, Eric. And thanks for the advice about Karly."

Eric grinned and grabbed one side of the rack. "If you'll help me drag *your* deer to *your* truck, the five of us will come over and eat up all *your* back straps just to say you're welcome. We'll be there at noon sharp with forks and knives in hand."

Eric, Lisa, and their three kids arrived at Joseph and Karly's place around noon. Eric parked at the curb. Just as Lisa exited the passenger side, she heard an airplane engine. After looking up, she said, "Hey Eric, kids, check out the plane circling overhead. Whoever is piloting that bird seems to be interested in this spot. I hope there's nothing wrong. Maybe there's a police chase going on in the area."

She glanced around and noticed that people were coming outside to observe the sight.

After a minute or so of climbing higher in the sky, the plane started making loops, leaving a trail of white in its wake.

"It's skywriting!" Lisa exclaimed.

Eric smiled when he saw the first letter the white smoke formed against the deep-blue background. He stood beside Lisa and put his arm around her shoulder. "Look! It's an 'I.' And I bet I know who the 'I' is. In fact, there he is, walking out the front door right now with Karly."

Joseph put his hand over his eyebrows as a shade from the sunlight as he looked up. He pointed up and looked at Karly.

As she raised her eyes toward the plane, she saw the plane finish a red heart that was floating next to the huge, well-defined "I."

Within a few minutes the entire message was hovering over the town for every citizen to see: "I ♥ U, KT" The pilot flew a little lower and then formed the letters "JT".

All the neighbors applauded as they looked over at Joseph and Karly.

Joseph turned to Karly and saw tears forming in her widened eyes. She was smiling and holding her hand over her heart. He reached for her hand and said, "I love you, Karly!"

Seeing Lisa's eyes tear up when she saw how much this aerial love letter meant to Karly, Eric gave his wife a big hug and stood beside her, relishing their closeness.

After a while people moved back into their houses, and Joseph and Karly greeted Lisa, Eric, and their kids. They moved inside and then went out the back door for the barbecue.

When Joseph was standing by the grill, Eric walked over and whispered, "Good job, man. You got her attention big time." Eric looked at the sky again. "Now that's what I call a fresh scrape!"

EIGHT

THE
DEBATE

Jim felt the weight of his compound bow as it dangled at the end of his pull-up string, but the intense darkness of the predawn woods prevented him from seeing it. He paused in his hand-over-hand retrieval. With his right forefinger and thumb he pinched the button embedded in the bill of his camo cap that turned on the built-in light.

The soft light made it easier to track the progress of the bow as he carefully hoisted it up. He knew if the limbs of his compound clanged against the platform of his aluminum climbing stand, any deer within earshot would know an intruder had entered their home. To keep them from getting spooked and leaving, Jim held the pull-up string as far out from the tree as he could while pulling it toward his feet.

With the bow safely in his left hand, Jim carefully sat down on the chair of his stand. He detached the pull-up string, rolled it into a tight ball, and then buried it in the thigh pocket of his pants. He quietly nocked an arrow on his string and scanned the woods. As the light gradually pierced the darkness, the stillness of the early morning amplified every sound in his surroundings. The most noticeable was the soft splat of dew droplets falling to the forest floor from the late-September leaves on the trees. There was no rhythm, but to Jim's ear it was sweet music.

"Man, I love this!" The words burst out in a controlled whisper. "And, Lord, thank You for this place I'm allowed to hunt on." The mountainside he was on was a 500-acre tract he'd hunted a couple of times near the end of the previous season. The property line extended from the road at the base of the mountain, where his truck was parked, to the backside of the ridge at the top. Mr. Hughes, the owner, was a farmer and client of Jim's insurance business. Only one other person had permission to hunt on the property—and that hunter's preference was using a rifle, so Jim had this entire area to himself during archery season. He stretched and felt his body and soul relax in the contentment and joy of being alone in the wilderness.

During his preseason scouting in July, Jim had found that deer had cut three major trails through these woods. He'd located his stand on a level flat a little over halfway up the mountain where the trails converged. Just as he'd hoped, the deer were still using those routes. Knowing more about the terrain this time around also clued Jim in on which direction the deer would most likely be moving during the morning hours. With every passing minute of growing daylight, his hopes for bagging a deer swelled.

Okay, boys and girls, it's time to get this show started! He waited patiently for the woods and animals to respond to his curtain call. About 20 minutes after the sun began it's slow climb above the eastern horizon, Jim heard the faint sound of wood snapping. Forgetting the heavy mugginess that had dampened his clothing and chilled the exposed skin around his collar, he swiveled his head.

"Yessss!" he whispered a little more loudly than he intended. Alert, he listened for more steps and searched the area in the direction the sound had come from. *This hunt could be over before Sheryl puts the coffee on this morning.* He slowly and quietly stood, but wisely kept the movement down by not turning to look around the tree. Jim carefully attached his string release and listened. His heart pounded.

He heard the soft sounds again. As the noise got closer and

more distinguishable, he realized something wasn't quite right. The cadence and heaviness of the steps weren't right for a deer. He keyed in on the growing sounds and finally made a disappointing assessment. *That sounds...human. And if it is human, whoever it is sure isn't in a hurry. And that guy is definitely going to mess with the deer traffic around here.*

Jim held on to the hope that his guess was wrong and put some tension on the string with his release. He fought the urge to rubberneck around the tree just in case his ears were playing tricks on him and it was indeed a deer. At last the sounds indicated the creature was passing close to his stand. He looked down slowly, keeping his movements slow and gentle.

Eighteen feet below him a stranger was moving through the woods. As Jim dealt with the reality that his hunt was in jeopardy, he kept quiet as the man walked past his stand. *Who is that? No bow or camo. What's he doing walking through this stretch of timber at this time of the morning? Maybe he's one of Mr. Hughes' kin I haven't met.* A quiet sigh escaped. *Big-time bummer for my hunt.*

As the man stepped carefully down one of the deer trails, Jim saw him look back over his shoulder several times, but the guy never looked up. Debating whether to speak to the stranger who obviously didn't know he had company, Jim's die-hard bow hunter instinct argued, *After all the effort and energy you've put into today, don't waste it. Let the guy walk. Maybe he hasn't scared all the deer away.*

Opting to salvage his morning by deliberately being unsociable, Jim made some quiet calculations. *If the guy keeps going at the pace he's moving, within 10 minutes this part of the woods will settle down again. Maybe I'll see a four-legged critter in spite of that guy.*

Sitting down again, Jim tried to focus on the hunt, but his attention kept drifting back and forth between the local deer population and a growing curiosity about the individual who had invaded his space. He replayed his mental film of the stranger's unexpected appearing, realizing more details about his demeanor and clothing.

His face. I'm thinking he looked a little nervous…and tired too.

The backpack…it wasn't large, but it did seem full. Maybe he wandered off the Appalachian Trail. I wonder if he was lost. Maybe I should've spoken up. Humph. Oh well.

And what was with those high-top boots?

He did have good taste in hats. Looked like my fishing cap.

I wonder where the guy was headed?

Suddenly Jim's right pants pocket vibrated. Startled, he retrieved his cell phone and flipped it open. "Hello." Jim kept his voice to a stealthy whisper.

"Jim, I'm sorry to bother you when you're on your stand."

"It's okay, babe. You sound tense. What's up?"

"You're at Mr. Hughes' place this morning, right?"

"Yes."

"So you're on the east side of the county and 20 miles or so from the far side of town?"

"Right. Why?"

"I got up about 15 minutes ago and turned on the radio. Do you remember the abortion clinic that was bombed over in Carson three weeks ago?"

"Yep."

"The police are pretty sure they know who did it, but they haven't been able to find the guy. This morning they announced they think they know where he's hiding. They said he's skilled as a survivalist and has disappeared into the mountains. Apparently a farmer saw someone fitting the man's description crossing Jamison Road yesterday evening near Wells Center."

"Jamison Road isn't too far from where I am right now. When I leave the main highway to get to Mr. Hughes' property, the road I turn onto is Jamison. Wells Center is the last community I go through before getting here. Mr. Hughes' farm is about three miles out from there."

Sheryl looked at the clock on the kitchen stove. "It's a little after

six thirty. I'm getting ready to pick up Mom for breakfast, and then I'm taking her to her doctor's appointment. You probably won't encounter the bomber, but for my peace of mind, will you check in with me from time to time today?"

"Sure, hon."

"Thanks, Jim. I feel better already. I'll talk to you…"

"Say, Sheryl, before you go, did you happen to get the description of the guy the cops are looking for?"

"Yes. They think he's wearing a brown leather jacket and jeans. In the drawing they showed, he was wearing a hat like the one you wear fishing. Oh, and they said he was wearing boots—possibly army boots."

"Thanks, Sheryl."

"Jim, they also said he might be armed and should be considered dangerous."

"Okay, Sheryl. I'll be fine, babe. And don't worry, I'll check in. Thanks for calling."

"I love you, Jim."

"I love you too. I'll talk to you later."

Jim slowly and quietly closed his phone. He carefully scanned the area around his stand, his thoughts racing.

That hiker sure matches that description. I can't believe he walked right below me. It's gotta be him.

Thank You, Lord, for keeping me quiet.

What should I do? Probably the best thing is to shimmy down the tree and make a beeline for the truck.

I'm an idiot! I've got the answer to this problem in my hand. I'll call the police! Duh!

Jim flipped the phone open and punched the 9. Before he entered another number he stopped. *What am I going to say? I need to think this through so they won't think I'm a kook.*

Having never made a call to a 9-1-1 operator, Jim quickly rehearsed his words. He kept his voice to a whisper. "Hello. This is Jim Teasly from Parsons. I'm hunting on a mountain near Wells Center. I'm on property owned by Garrett Hughes. Right now I'm in my tree stand. A few minutes ago a fellow walked by on a…"

Jim stopped mid-rehearsal. His stomach tightened as he caught a glimpse of the man's figure moving through the undergrowth to his left, coming toward his tree stand.

He slowly lowered the bright silver cell phone to his thigh, folding it gently closed. *Please don't look up, mister.*

A mere 150 feet from his tree, the man stopped next to a young oak. It was the same guy who had passed by before. He leaned his shoulder against the tree and rested.

Jim was grateful to see quite a bit of foliage on the low-hanging branches between him and the intruder. He hoped that the clumps of leaves and his camo clothing would be enough to conceal him from the fellow's eyes. He didn't move a muscle.

After what seemed like an hour but was probably only a few minutes, the man below Jim pushed himself away from the oak and stepped slightly around the tree. Facing away from the tree stand, he lowered his body to a cross-legged seated position.

He leaned forward and slipped off his backpack. He massaged his neck and shoulders with both hands and then dropped his head between his knees. After three or four minutes he raised his head and then leaned back against the tree, shutting his eyes.

At least he's facing away from me. He looks tired—tired enough that maybe he'll go to sleep. If he does, I can climb down quietly and move far enough away to call 9-1-1.

Climbing down might be too dangerous. It might be best to just dial the police and see if I can let them know where I'm at without waking the hiker.

I sure wish the wind would pick up and give me some sound and movement as additional cover. He looked toward the sky and silently added, *Lord, how about it? Will You kick up the wind a little? You've been known to calm it. How about stirring it up this time?*

Jim waited for an answer to his prayer, but the air remained hauntingly still. Convinced that the stranger was the bomber, he stared at the man's profile and wondered what could have possessed him to bomb the abortion clinic.

Maybe he's had it rough. Maybe his dad beat him up or threw him out. Maybe he's in a gang. Or maybe it's none of that. Perhaps the guy believes abortion shouldn't be allowed and decided to take matters into his own hands.

As Jim silently contemplated that maybe the man's reason for bombing the clinic was his antiabortion stance, another thought gripped him. *Well, Lord, You know I don't believe abortion is right. I know I'm on Your side about this issue. How can we be a "nation under God" if we're killing the most innocent among us?*

Jim forced himself to stop analyzing the situation long enough to slowly look around the area. Seeing nothing out of the ordinary, he looked back at the man leaning against the oak. *Sure looks like he's asleep. I'm going to make that call.*

Covering the bright silver phone with his palm, Jim flipped it open. He quickly double-checked to make sure it was in silent mode and started to push the numbers. He paused when a challenging thought hit him. *Do I really want to be the one to tell the cops where this guy is? Think about what he did. How many times has it crossed my mind that someone should do something to shut down that place? I'd love to see every clinic like that in the nation shut down and have every doctor who does abortions go out of business. This guy had the guts to do something about it. He did what a lot of people want to do... but don't have the nerve.*

Jim took a deep, slow breath as he assimilated what had just entered his mind. Realizing he'd worked himself into an emotional lather, he engaged in some necessary self-coaching. *I've got to calm down. I can't be that fellow's cheerleader. What he did wasn't right. Two wrongs don't make a right. Killing babies is wrong, but so is bombing a building. He could've killed someone. He's a bona fide criminal, and*

I'll be an accomplice if I choose not to contact the authorities. What good is the law if it doesn't apply to everyone? God is in charge of vengeance. And He says He'll take care of it.

Jim slowly pushed the buttons, making sure the silver phone was hidden behind his hand. Moving slower than a shadow on a sundial, he raised the flip phone to his ear.

"9-1-1 operator. What is your emergency?"

With his hand cupped around the mouthpiece to suppress the sound, he softly whispered, "Can you hear me? If you can, would you whisper back to me?"

The operator replied, her voice lowered. "Yes, sir. What is your emergency?"

"My name is Jim Teasly. I'm hunting on the property of Garrett Hughes near Wells Center. I believe I'm looking at the man who bombed the abortion clinic in Carson. I'm about 150 feet away and 18 feet above him in a tree stand. He hasn't seen me yet. He's sitting at the base of a tree, and I think he might be...well, I'm hoping he's asleep at the moment."

"Hang on, please. I'm contacting the state police and FBI. Does the man have any weapons visible?"

"I don't see any, but that doesn't mean he doesn't have them. If he hears me or sees me, I'll be in big trouble."

Accompanied by the clicking of keys on a keyboard, the operator continued, "What's your cell phone number? And is it GPS enabled?"

Jim gave her the information and said he thought it was.

"You say you're hunting? What weapons do you have with you?"

"I'm a bow hunter."

"Mr. Teasly, please describe the man you have in your sights."

Jim's adrenal glands went into overtime as he nervously responded, "He's wearing jeans, heavy calf-high army boots, a brown leather jacket, and a round-bill hat."

"Please stay on the line. I won't talk to you unless I have to. Do everything you can to avoid a confrontation. Do you understand?"

"Yes. If you need more information about me or my location, my wife, Sheryl, is at my home number. " He gave her his home address and number.

"We're pinpointing where you are. Several ground units are on their way. They estimate their arrival in the area will be 20 minutes. We're also dispatching a helicopter that's nearby. In 10 minutes… maybe less…you'll hear it approaching. The man you're watching will hear it too, so be careful. Please stay on the line and tell me if he moves. I'll need to know what direction he goes."

"Got it."

"And Mr. Teasly, stay put and stay quiet. Don't try to detain him or distract him."

Knowing help was on its way, Jim tried to relax. His muscles, tense from strain, were aching. His back, rear, and legs were feeling abused from staying in one position so long. Afraid that even a slight shift in position might cause something on his aluminum stand to squeak or pop, he forced his body to remain motionless and gave himself a pep talk.

Fight it, Jimbo. Hang on for 10 more minutes. Think about how glad you are that you kept your trap shut when this guy walked under your stand a while ago.

Suddenly Jim caught the low rumbling sound of an approaching helicopter. He looked up but only saw small pieces of sky through the trees. He glanced back at the stranger. He was raising his head and looking around. A horrible thought clicked in Jim's mind. He pressed the phone close to his mouth. "Ma'am, I hear the chopper in the distance, and it's closing in pretty quick. The man below me hears it too. He's getting agitated. He's going to be scanning the sky any second now. What if he sees me?"

"Let's hope he doesn't. But if he does, defend yourself."

"Okay. Since I'm a bow hunter, I need to put the phone away in case I need to grab my gear."

The operator paused. "Okay. Set the phone down, but leave the line open, okay?"

"Will do."

Leaving the phone unfolded, he placed it next to him on the climber's seat, making sure it was secure. With as much finesse as he could gather, Jim slowly stood, hoping the chopper noise would divert the guy's eyes and ears from his direction. Ten seconds later, his body deeply grateful to have finally moved, he was ready. He attached the release to his string and rested the lower wheel of his bow at his beltline. It was the same position he took when preparing to shoot a deer. The idea that his target was human made his blood run cold.

If he looks my way and sees me, I don't have a choice. But I'm not going to make a move unless I see a weapon.

As the helicopter got closer and closer, Jim felt the thumping air pressure of the rotors. Suddenly he saw the chopper! It hovered about a 100 feet above the treetops just slightly to his left. Jim smiled as he suddenly realized God had answered his prayer about stirring up the wind. The chaotic movement of the tree branches and leaves was all the protection he'd need to safely raise his bow to shooting position.

Looking down, Jim saw the man sling his pack onto his back and take off. He detached his release and reached for the cell phone.

"Ma'am, the man took off. He's headed east."

"Copy. Don't hang up yet. Officers are on the hillside, heading toward your location. Be careful and stay alert. The suspect might see them and turn back toward you. Let me know if you see him."

Jim kept the phone to his ear and listened for commotion on the ground. The sound of the chopper engine and the wash of wind from the blades blocked almost everything. He checked the woods carefully. All at once, coming back down the flat, Jim caught sight

of the fugitive hightailing it toward his stand. He whispered into the phone, "He's back!" Then he quickly stuffed the open phone into his pocket, reattached his release, and came to full draw.

When the man approached the tree where he'd been resting just a few minutes before, Jim carefully looked at the fugitive's hands. Not seeing a weapon, Jim decided to act.

"Hey!" he yelled at the top of his lungs.

The stranger slid to a halt and looked around rapidly. He turned, looking in a full circle. Not thinking to look up and with the chopper noise making it hard to pinpoint the direction Jim's voice was coming from, the guy hesitated.

Jim wasn't sure what the police would really say in this situation, but he'd seen enough cop shows that he figured he could borrow a line or two.

"Lay down on the ground and put your hands on the back of your head. Do it now!"

The stranger suddenly looked straight up at Jim. His face froze and his mouth hung open. He dropped to his knees. Still staring at the arrow aimed at his chest, he put his hands on the ground and lowered his body to the forest floor. He put his hands behind his head.

"Lace your fingers together," Jim ordered. "And don't move."

In less than a minute, Jim saw well-armed police officers approaching. He yelled, "Hey! Up here! Your suspect is lying on the ground by my tree stand."

As the officers arrived and cuffed the intruder, Jim pointed his bow away from the growing crowd and released the tension on his string. He heard the chopper gain altitude and fly toward Carson.

In the welcomed quiet, one officer looked up at Jim. "According to the 9-1-1 operator, you must be Jim Teasly."

"Yes, sir. I'm really glad to see you guys."

"You bet. You've been a big help. It's safe to come down now."

Jim lowered the bow and sat down on his climber chair. "Give me a minute to catch my breath, okay?"

"Sure. I understand." The officer put his hands on his hips. "I'm thinking your deer hunt is over for the day, Mr. Teasly. You certainly bagged a big one today."

"Thanks. Is it okay if I make a quick phone call? I need to let my wife know I'm okay. The 9-1-1 operator may have called her, so she'll be worried."

"Go ahead."

As he pushed the speed dial number for Sheryl's phone and waited for her to answer, three officers escorted the suspect past the tree stand and headed down the trail. When they were just a few yards away, the fugitive looked up at Jim. Their gazes locked. In that unforgettable moment Jim saw exhaustion in the man's eyes and wondered if he saw relief as well. *I wonder what that guy sees in my eyes?* Jim thought.

⇾ NINE ⇽

TRADITION

K im closed her cell phone and walked to the window of her dormitory room. As she looked out across the lawn of the college campus, she replayed the conversation she'd just had with her dad.

"Kim! How's my little kitten?"

"Fine, Dad, and you and Mom?"

"We're enjoying the cool weather. I've got to tell you, the frost on the ground this morning got me thinking extra hard about muzzleloader season. It starts in a month."

Kim knew where he was heading with his report. She thought about how she'd responded halfheartedly with an "uh-huh" to her dad's obvious excitement. While she hoped he hadn't noticed her less-than-enthusiastic response, in retrospect she realized he was more subdued when he continued the conversation. She could tell he was concerned that a break in their long-enjoyed tradition might be looming.

"Well, I suspect you're swamped with all the freshman work you're dealing with at the university, but I'm hoping you'll want to come home on opening weekend to go out to the woods with me. I have a stand tied up in a tree down in Three Pond Hollow."

Kim gave the safest answer she could think of. "I'll think about it, Dad."

There was a detectable upswing in her father's tone. "That's great, Kim! I'll make sure the stand is in good shape. And I'll tune in your .50 caliber so if you come everything will be ready."

Kim didn't have the heart to reveal her reservations about going deer hunting with her dad this year. And she wasn't ready to discuss why yet. To hide her feelings she turned the conversation his way, hoping to squelch the worry she heard in his voice.

"Thanks, Dad. I have a feeling you'll not only check the stands and zero in the smoke pole, but you're also going to wash my camo and marinate them in leaves for that all-important scent suppression, right?"

"You bet, Kim! I'll do all that, plus I'll make sure you're legal. Your tag won't cost you a dime this year. It's my treat."

As her dad continued the list of what he planned to do to be ready for her arrival for the hunt, Kim could feel her resistance to returning to the woods for deer hunting draining from her heart like water from a punctured barrel. Still, she wasn't ready to commit to the excursion yet. She decided to give herself one last chance to back out by delaying her final decision.

"I do have to check my exam schedule, Dad. I'll call you in a few days and let you know if I can come. Please tell Mom I said hi. And Dad..." Kim paused. "Thanks for thinking of me."

"Sure thing, Kim. I figured you could use a break from classes. I know I could sure use some daughter time. You're still my best huntin' buddette!"

As the late-afternoon sun filtered through the dorm window and warmed Kim's face, she quietly listed the possible reasons she could give to pass on the hunt this year without hurting her dad's feelings.

Maybe there will be a test I have to study for. Or maybe one of my friends will need some help. The rehearsal date for the choir might be changed to that Saturday...

On the other side of the state, Kim's mother interrupted her husband's pensive stare. "Turner, you've been sitting there and gazing at the wall for a long time. What's on your mind?"

Turner pursed his lips and slowly shook his head from side to side. He looked at his wife. "Well, Ellen, I just talked to Kim and asked if she would like to come home for opening day of muzzle-loader season."

"And the conversation didn't go as you'd hoped?"

Turner rubbed the back of his neck.

Ellen knew that when his hand went to his neck while he talked, his state of mind was somewhere between confused and worried.

"Well, I didn't get a no. She said she'd check her exam schedule and then call and let me know. I was expecting her to be all over the idea like a kid with a dish of ice cream." Turner sighed long. "Ellen, I'm wondering if something's happening to my girl's feelings about hunting."

Seeing the hurt and concern on her husband's face, she tried to lift his spirits with a slice of female intuition. "Come on, Turner. Kim's not going to pass on opening day. Plus, you two have a long tradition of going hunting together. You've been doing it since she was 10 years old! She might be a little distracted with studies and everything else that goes with her first year at college, but the dropping temperatures, the aroma of fallen leaves, and all the other things that herald hunting season will bring her home. Besides, she loves being with her dad in the woods. That'll do the job quicker than anything."

Turner pushed himself up and out of his recliner, picked up his empty coffee cup, and headed to the kitchen.

Ellen waited for a sign that he'd heard and was encouraged by her comments.

"You're probably right, honey, just like always," Turner said as he entered the kitchen.

Ellen whispered, "I sure hope so."

Nearly a week passed before Kim called her dad. He was standing on the platform of one of his tall, homemade wooden ladder stands when his phone chirped. He pulled the phone from his pocket and checked the screen. His heart raced at the sight of Kim's name.

"Hi, Kim. How's my little kitten?"

Kim felt a bit guilty realizing she was glad her dad's sentimental greeting and pet name for her were only audible to her.

"Doing fine, Dad. And you?"

"At this very moment I'm standing on top of the world at the head of Three Pond Hollow. I'm safe and sound on the platform of the ladder stand up here, and it's still healthy enough to hold both of us." He looked out through the woods as he steeled himself for the bad news he was afraid Kim would share. He felt like a man sitting in a doctor's office waiting for the results of a test for cancer.

More than 200 miles away, just like a week earlier, the courage Kim had worked up to break the news to her dad that she wasn't going to come home for the first day of hunting season vanished at the sound of her dad's voice. Her well-rehearsed speech gave way to impulsive words she knew would be music to his ears. "Seeing any good signs around that stand this year, Dad?"

Turner grinned at the implications but tried to contain his excitement. "Oh, you know Three Pond Hollow. It's still an interstate system for deer like it has been for more than 100 years. I saw a rub on a tree that was nearly as big as the columns on the front porch of our house! Well, at least half as big around."

"That's big, Dad! Sounds like that ten-point I missed last year survived the season. I still can't believe my shot went wide at only 90 yards."

Turner sat down on the seat of the ladder stand. "It sure is great to talk to you, kitten. It almost feels like you're right here with me. And why on earth would we go deer hunting if it didn't generate the kind of excitement that blurs our vision and makes our hands shake a little sometimes?"

Kim laughed with her dad at his statement he'd used through the years when "buck fever" caused her to miss the mark. She smiled at how the familiar words brought lingering comfort. Then she remembered her reason for calling. But her decision to not go was being transcended by the enthusiasm and joy in her dad's voice. For a brief moment she debated about sticking to her plan, but it was so much easier and felt a lot better to revamp her plans.

"Well, make sure my .50 cal is in the small circle 'cause if that buck shows up on opening day, I'm going to show you how it's done."

Turner pumped his arm. "Okay, Kim! I'm so glad you're coming! And, young lady, you just might get a chance to redeem yourself. I'll do my part, you do yours, and we'll hope that buck does his. And what have I always said?"

Kim knew the answer to her dad's question, and she knew that giving it would settle the matter of whether or not she was going home for the hunt. "Must be present to win!" she replied.

"That's right, kitten. And I look forward to hunting with you. It's tradition, you know."

Kim said goodbye, listened to her dad's goodbyes, and closed her cell phone.

"I can't believe you caved!"

Kim whipped around and stared at her roommate. "You startled me, Wendy. I didn't hear you come in. I know I caved, but you didn't hear my dad's voice. I just didn't have the heart to disappoint him. He's so excited about going hunting with me."

Wendy cocked her hip and shot back, "Your dad—and anyone else who hunts—is a killer, Kim. And you're going to let him keep making one out of you? I thought you decided to save the life of a deer instead of taking one."

"My dad is not a killer, Wendy. He's a hunter. There's a *huge* difference between the two."

"Yeah, right, Kimberly. Your dad is murdering defenseless deer that aren't a threat to anyone. He's taking the lives of innocent, harmless creatures. And so is anyone else who hunts."

Kim heard the echoes of the argument she and Wendy had engaged in a few weeks earlier. Wendy had been shocked when she discovered Kim was an avid hunter. And since then, on several occasions, heated conversations had erupted on the issue. But this was the first time Wendy had used the word "murder."

"Herod the Great, Nero, Hitler, Jack the Ripper, Ted Bundy, Saddam Hussein—those are murderers, Wendy. There is no justification whatsoever for their despicable crimes. Putting people who hunt animals for food in that category is ludicrous. You're implying that an animal has the same attributes and purposes as a human. Humans and animals are different in kind. No matter how hard you try to give animals the virtues and rights you and I have, it's not going to happen."

Wendy ran both her hands through her black hair before putting them on her hips. "I…"

"To prove my point, Wendy, a mature whitetail buck might impregnate up to a dozen females during mating season. He goes from one doe to another, doing what he was designed to do. Does that sound like a relationship garnering trait? What do you think of that bit of news?"

"Not much, but…"

"By 'not much,' do you mean you haven't thought about it or are you saying the buck has poor character?"

"No," Wendy huffed. "I mean I don't assign any judgment to his mating habits."

"My point exactly! You, me, and most of the human world believe male deer are acting natural when they 'service' multiple females. Now, what would you do if you heard that your boyfriend, Marcus— the guy who has you wrapped around his little finger—has 'visited' the beds of a dozen women since he's been on campus. What would you think about that revelation?"

"I'd be outraged, obviously."

Kim picked up her Bible from her bed. She turned pages as she continued her conversation. "Why would you be upset?"

Wendy flipped her hair out of her eyes. "Well, everyone knows that sleeping around is just, well, wrong."

Kim stopped leafing through her Bible, put her forefinger between two pages, and held the book closed as she went on. "Where did you get the idea that a guy on this campus—or anywhere else for that matter—going from the bed of one gal to another and another is wrong?"

"I…I…well…er…I…uh, I guess I don't actually know."

Kim opened her Bible. "Listen to this, Wendy. This is from the book of Romans, chapter 2, verse 15: 'They show the work of the law written in their hearts, their conscience bearing witness and their thoughts alternately accusing or else defending them.' According to this, you and I have God's laws—His standards—written in our hearts. In essence we bear the watermark of God. In your spirit and mine is a God-given, unique ability to sense the difference between right and wrong. We sense God's values and apply them to our world. Animals don't have this gift. That old buck going from doe to doe doesn't feel one ounce of regret or guilt about his exploits. He doesn't even think about it. And the females he visits aren't going to hang out in the woods crying and carrying on when he goes to the next doe because they feel used, violated, or abused."

Wendy's mouth hung slightly open as she took in Kim's logic.

"And I can confidently say that if Marcus were doing with women what that buck does with his harem, somewhere deep inside him he knows his behavior isn't acceptable. And if he doesn't, it's because his conscience has been hardened by habitually feeding his lust and buying into the errant beliefs of today's culture. Even then, his actions will catch up with him sooner or later, and he'll face and feel the consequences. And you know that most women who

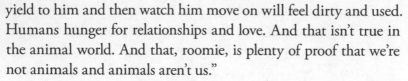

yield to him and then watch him move on will feel dirty and used. Humans hunger for relationships and love. And that isn't true in the animal world. And that, roomie, is plenty of proof that we're not animals and animals aren't us."

Wendy slowly sat down on her bed and folded her hands in her lap. She frowned slightly and stared at the floor.

"Wendy, I care about you and value your opinion. I don't want to come across as mean-spirited, but for several weeks I've listened to your forceful opinions about the evils of hunting, and I needed to let you know my side. And when you called my dad a murderer, that was going too far. Yes, there are plenty of unethical hunters out there who make the rest of us look bad, and I know a few of them. They give plenty of ammunition to those who oppose hunting. But there are hunters like my dad and me who are ethical from head to toe. We do care about animals, and when we take an animal, we don't waste the meat and we make the kill as clean and fast as possible. We don't want them to suffer any more than necessary. I'm proud of Dad. He taught me good hunting ethics and values. And even if you don't change your mind about hunting, take my dad and me, and other careful hunters, off your criminal list."

Kim took a deep breath and waited for Wendy to say something. "I've given you a lot to think about, I know. And in a way, I'm glad you challenged me about hunting. You made me really think about what I believe in. In fact, your challenge almost convinced me to abandon two of my most favorite things in the world to do—be with my dad and hunt. I love my dad, I like to hunt, and I'm an unapologetic omnivore."

Wendy looked up at her roommate. "No harm done, Kim. You have a right to your opinions. And, honestly, you've presented your side of the issue quite well. Your point about how humans are on a higher plane in terms of values and sensitivities is something I've never really considered. That caught me by surprise."

Kim sat down on her bed and quietly allowed the air to settle in the room. As she observed her friend's body language, she noticed Wendy was wringing her hands.

"Wendy, something else seems to be going on in your head besides our differences about hunting. Do you want to talk about it?"

Wendy didn't look up, but she started talking through quiet sobs. "All of a sudden there are two or three thoughts fighting for first place in my head. I'm not sure which one needs the most attention. I'm confused."

Kim reached across the narrow room and tapped Wendy lightly on the knee. "Just throw one at me, and we'll start there."

"You don't mind?"

"Nope. Toss me one."

Wendy took a deep breath. "No one has ever told me that God made us with His values written on our hearts. If that's true, that must be why I've been bothered when I've done some things that didn't seem so bad at the time but later have haunted me. And it seemed like everyone around me didn't think my actions were a problem either."

Kim nodded, encouraging Wendy to continue.

"That really hit me in the heart."

"In a good way though, right?"

Wendy looked out the dorm window and answered slowly, "Yes. Definitely yes."

"God's Word has a way of doing that. It cuts through the hard bones of resistance and pierces the spirit. His truth can literally change your life for the better. Even the fact that you recognize there is truth in God's Word is one more sign of our uniqueness. Animals will never know that kind of discovery. It's kind of sad in a way."

Wendy smiled and reached for a tissue in the box on the nightstand next to her bed. She wiped her eyes.

"You said there were several things battling for your attention. What's the next one?"

Taking another deep breath, Wendy exhaled and then said, "I'm

bothered by something I've done, and I don't like feeling that way. Especially because it didn't seem so bad before, but now I'm thinking it is. I don't like that either."

Kim furrowed her brows as she tried to understand Wendy's comments. Then she slowly smiled. "Oh, Wendy! That's really profound. You totally get it. What you just said may sound odd, but it's totally biblical. There's a verse in 2 Corinthians about that very idea."

Kim sat back and opened her Bible to the verse. "It's from chapter 7, verse 10: 'They show the work of the Law written in their hearts, their conscience bearing witness and their thoughts alternately accusing or else defending them.' In other words, godly sorrow, that's the sadness you feel when you've done something that goes against God's values, gives you the chance to realize you're sorry. And if you're sorry for what you've done, you can tell God and ask for His forgiveness. That's called repentance. And that can lead to salvation, which is accepting God's forgiveness offered through His Son, Jesus."

Kim closed her Bible. "I don't know what you've done that makes you feel bad but..."

Wendy held her hand up.

Kim stopped talking and looked at her questioningly.

"The word is 'dirty,' Kim. I don't just feel bad, I feel dirty. In fact, 'filthy' describes it even better."

Kim sat back on her bed and looked understandingly at Wendy. Suspecting what was implied by "dirty," Kim got up, moved to Wendy's bed, and sat down beside her. "I think I understand what you're getting at Wendy," she said gently. "And I won't think any less of you no matter what it is. And even better than that is that God loves you. He understands people—He understands you. He won't hate you. In fact, He'll do everything possible to help you. He gave us our ability to be sensitive to His ways and values. And He enables us to feel sorrow when we violate those ways so we can be sorry and turn to Him for comfort and healing. So feeling bad about the not-so-great things you've done is a good thing. The uncomfortable feeling isn't your enemy; it's your friend. It's the very thing that can turn you toward God. And God wants you to have a close relationship with Him."

Wendy assimilated what Kim told her.

"Okay, Kim. Let me get this straight. You're saying that if I feel bad for something I've done that has made me feel dirty, I should be glad I feel bad because the feeling bad let's me know I need to talk to God about it. And if I talk to Him and tell Him I'm sorry, He'll help me feel better. Right?"

Kim's head went sideways and her eyes shifted back and forth as she absorbed Wendy's interpretation of their conversation. Jumping to her feet, Kim turned, grabbed Wendy's hands, and pulled her up. "Yes! You've got it! You're not the animal you thought you were."

Wendy reacted with a puzzled laugh at first, and then it dawned on her what Kim meant. She hugged Kim and then stepped back. "Who would've ever thought I'd learn anything from a kill…uh…I mean…hunter."

"How about that! And I never ever thought I'd hug an animal rights activist. My dad isn't going to believe this."

"Speaking of your dad, I'm sorry I called him a murderer. I went overboard, and I didn't realize how it would sound. I've heard that extreme rhetoric a lot at the campus meetings and in the pamphlets, so I guess I just repeated what I've taken in. We animal activists can get pretty radical when it comes to our agendas."

Kim rolled her eyes. "No kidding."

"When I got to campus it was easy to find a group of students who supported animal rights. I felt very comfortable with them. But I didn't expect to be sharing my dorm room with a hunter—with someone who did what I've always hated. You've put a face on the 'nameless' hunters. I still don't like the idea of killing anything, but I have a better understanding of where you're coming from. You've listened to me and my views, and I appreciate that."

"Thanks, Wendy. We don't have to agree. We can agree to disagree."

Kim went to her desk and gathered her books for her next class. She shoved them into her backpack and glanced at her watch. "I have time for one more of those thoughts swirling in your head if you want to share more."

"I'll be quick because we both have classes to go to." Wendy sighed deeply. "The short version is that I envy what you have with your dad."

Kim turned and looked at Wendy. "What?"

"Every time I hear you talking to your dad on the phone—and it seems to be pretty often—"

"I know. Dad calls a lot. It's a bit embarrassing."

Wendy put her hand on Kim's arm, "Oh, Kim, don't be embarrassed. I think it's great your dad wants a relationship with you."

Kim saw tears forming in Wendy's eyes.

"I've never known that kind of love," Wendy continued. "I'm not sure my dad even remembers where he dropped me off for college. I'd give anything to be to my dad what you are to yours."

Kim watched the drops fall off of Wendy's cheeks. She extended her arms and invited Wendy in for a consoling embrace. As they were heart to heart, Kim closed her eyes and visualized her dad's face. A sudden swell of gratitude for the boundless love of her father washed over her like a tidal wave.

"Wendy, I'm so sorry you don't have with your dad what I have with mine. My dad and I have been very close for years."

Wendy backed away from Kim and went to her desk. She grabbed her backpack and put two books and a notebook inside. "As smart as you are, I'm surprised you didn't catch on that our worst arguments about hunting were right after I heard you talking to your dad. I was so jealous that I didn't want you to have what I've wanted for so long. I'm sorry, Kim. Will you forgive me for being so selfish?"

"I'm sorry you've felt that way. I do forgive you, Wendy. And I'll pray that you and your dad will find a way to connect. Is there something he likes to do that you could do with him?"

The two young women put on their coats and grabbed their backpacks. They stepped out the door, closing it behind them. Side-by-side they walked toward the elevator.

"My dad loves to fish," Wendy said. "But I've pretty much been a makeup and shopping mall type of daughter. Fishing is way too stinky and gory as far as I'm concerned. I'm not sure if I could go that far for him."

"So your dad likes to jerk innocent fish out of the water and let them suffocate."

Wendy stopped abruptly. "You are kidding, aren't you?"

"Yes. Yes, I am."

They both laughed as they continued down the hall and entered the elevator. Kim pushed the first-floor button and turned to Wendy. "Why don't you call your dad in the next day or two and ask him if you can go fishing with him. Once he gets over the shock, he might be really happy to do that with you."

The elevator stopped, the door opened, and Kim and Wendy stepped out. As they walked to the front door, Kim said, "And if the idea of fishing is too hard to contemplate, why not go with him and talk with him while he fishes?"

"I'll think about it," Wendy answered, opening the door for both of them. "See you later." She turned right and headed to her class.

As Kim turned left toward the science building, she took her cell phone out of her coat pocket and dialed her dad's number.

"Hello, kitten."

"Hey, Dad. I only have a minute because I'm on my way to class, but I wanted to thank you."

"For what, Kim?"

"Do you remember a couple of seasons ago when you told me how God had wired animals and humans differently? And that God gave humans something He didn't give animals? That each of us has a spirit that connects with God? You used a buck during rut season as an illustration."

"Yes, I remember that conversation. I was a bit worried that the illustration was too graphic, but it was the best explanation I knew. What brought that up?"

"Today I borrowed your analogy to help my roommate understand the difference between animals and humans. She was giving me grief about hunting, so I shared your illustration and the verse in Romans you used. She has a better understanding of hunting now, but even more important is that I think she's starting to figure out that she is a special creation of God...that she has the 'watermark of God on her spirit,' like you explained to me.

"So I called to let you know that I do listen to you, and that the time we spent together has helped me open up a conversation about God with Wendy. I also wanted to ask you and Mom to pray for Wendy with me.

"And Dad, I'm really looking forward to keeping our tradition in a couple of weeks. I can't wait to get out into the woods and do the fair chase with you. I've got to go. I'm walking into my class. Love you! Bye."

Turner pushed the red button on his cell phone and grinned as he put it in his shirt pocket. He pushed the safety button to off on the .50 caliber he was holding. Looking through the scope he centered the crosshairs on the black dot in the small circle of the paper target 100 yards away. He whispered, "God, bless my little kitten. And do bless her friend, Wendy." He ended his prayer with an amen and pulled the trigger.

Wendy pushed the green send button on her cell phone and pressed in a phone number. She put the phone to her ear and listened to the ringing. She heard a click and a hello. "Hi, Dad. It's Wendy. I, well, I was wondering..."

TEN

OLD
IRONSIGHTS

MMerle couldn't believe how noisy he was being. The dry leaves crunched loudly under his boots as he hiked on a Pennsylvania hillside. He tried to lessen the commotion of his entry into the woods, but nature was winning the decibel war. With each step announcing his presence to every deer in the area, he acknowledged the good possibility that his morning hunt might turn out to be a nice, quiet, therapeutic sit. Normally the likelihood of no action would bother him, but on this day another matter was preying on his mind. Some time to think was exactly what he needed. The problem had to do with the long-time friend cradled tightly in his arms.

In the low light of predawn he reached the familiar old red oak where he'd stood vigil so many times since his early teen years. He unfolded his collapsible stool and placed it as close as he could to the wide trunk. Making sure it was steady, he turned around and sat down. He loosened his grip on the .32 Winchester Special and laid it across his lap as he leaned back against the tree. After catching his breath from the 30-minute trek up the hill, Merle sighed deeply. He looked up through the leafless branches silhouetted against the sky that had turned blue-gray and prayerfully whispered, "God, You know how much I love this place. I give You my sincere thanks for letting me come to it again." As he said a heartfelt "Amen," Merle's grip tightened on the rifle in almost a stranglehold.

"I'm sorry, Old Ironsights," he said as he relaxed his grip. His mind went back through the years to when he'd reached the ripe young age of 14.

Merle remembered walking into the local hardware store in May of that year. Without a background check or answering a single legal question, he'd put a layaway payment on the counter for the Winchester. As the store owner counted the cash, Merle promised, "Mr. Adams, I'll be back with the rest of it before summer is over."

When early August came, Merle headed back to the hardware store with a stack of bills that were mostly hard-earned, although a few were hard-begged. The dollars that were the toughest to collect were the ones he'd gotten when he sold his favorite bicycle. Though giving up his fat-tire Schwinn wasn't easy, the anticipation of owning the brand-new rifle helped his affection for the old bike fade.

Mr. Adams smiled when he saw the teenager come through the entrance. "I see you've kept your promise. Are you taking the Winchester home with you today?"

"You bet I am, Mr. Adams!" Merle plopped the cash down on the counter, added his high-caliber smile, and said, "Thanks so much for holding it for me. I also need two boxes of shells."

"You're certainly welcome. Do you want me to put a scope on this fine piece, young man?"

"No, sir. I was doing well to come up with the dollars I needed for the gun and the shells."

Mr. Adams responded with the certain tone of experienced salesmanship, "Wouldn't be but another $35 for a pretty good 3 x 9. Seeing as how you're a man of your word, I could mount one for you, and you could pay me when you can."

Merle thought about the idea. "That's a mighty tempting offer, Mr. Adams. But I'd better wait. Maybe someday I can add a scope, but for now it's gonna be just me and..."

Merle paused mid-sentence.

Mr. Adams had lifted the .32 Winchester out of the long, cardboard box. He held it up to the light so it glistened on the wood stock and showed off the metal workmanship. He handed it to his young customer.

"Sounds like you've named this gun already. What did you choose?"

Like a proud papa would name his first child, Merle threw his shoulders back and answered, "Old Ironsights. That's what I'm gonna name him. Saw it in a book I read once, and it's as good a name as any for this beauty."

The cash-and-carry exchange was over in minutes, but the relationship begun that day between Merle and Old Ironsights promised to last a lifetime.

As soon as he got home, Merle began a prehunt ritual that he would repeat often through the years. After putting on his hunting clothes in the utility room at his folks' house, he picked up the Winchester and whispered, "Well, Old Ironsights, let's go huntin'!" It felt good and natural to speak to the gun, to his hunting buddy.

With that he pushed the squeaky screen door open, and almost before the slinky, rusted spring pulled the door closed, the excited teenager and his friend were almost at the tree line at the base of the hill about 50 yards behind the house.

Eventually the prehunt ritual altered slightly when Merle married Peggy. They bought their own little home close to his family's place, so now he dressed for the hunt in his own house and had to drive a bit to get to his favorite hunting spot.

But this morning had been different. For the first time in 15 years, Merle's prehunt ritual lacked enthusiasm. This time when he quietly spoke to his Winchester, there was a noticeable reserve in his voice.

As the late-November sun rose and the woods gradually let in the light, Merle reluctantly faced the reality of what was coming. He uneasily calculated the number of days left before December 25 arrived. "Only 28 days. Time's running out. If I'm going to do this, I'm gonna have to do it really soon."

Merle slid his left glove gently down the length of the Winchester, patted the barrel near the forward sight, and then gently said, "It hasn't been a good year for me business-wise, Ironsights. Actually it's been a dismal bust. There have been some unexpected things to cover, and what's worse, I don't see the situation gettin' much better in the months to come." With his right hand Merle patted the honey-colored wooden stock that boasted its share of deep scratches and telltale signs of being well used and loved.

"You know I don't want to do this to you, old buddy, but I've got those three little boys down there at the house who deserve a good Christmas. And the only way I can see gettin' them the things I've picked out for them is if I go through with this. I can't believe I even put the ad in the paper. I feel terrible, but it's the only choice I have. Today might be the end of the line for you and me, old friend."

Merle looked up and checked the surrounding area for movement. Then he looked at Old Ironsights again as tears welled up in his eyes. "You've been a faithful friend. Never gave me a minute's trouble. And boy do we have some history. But it seems it's time for me to let you go."

Merle felt somewhat foolish when he looked up again, this time to see if anyone happened to be nearby. *Good grief, man, do you realize you're talking to a gun? You're getting teary-eyed over a rifle? Yes, but...*

He hoped no one was close enough to hear his one-sided conversation. An hour passed. While looking for game, Merle debated whether he should cut his hunt short, head on home, and make the call to the man who had responded to his ad. Before he talked himself out of going through with the sale, he decided to gather his things to make the long descent down the hill to his truck.

Just as he stood, he saw a flash of brown about 150 yards through the openness of the timber to his right and below him. He stared and made out a small herd of deer hurrying up the hillside. Merle guessed they were probably escaping the neighboring Johnson boys, who seemed to always be late getting to the woods on a hunting day.

As the four whitetails quick-stepped onto the flat below him, Merle slowly raised the Winchester to his shoulder. If the deer stayed their course, he figured they would come by him at about 70 yards, moving right to left. His opportunity to touch off a shot would come in about 20 seconds.

With the stock plate of the .32 resting solidly on his right shoulder, he tenderly laid his jaw on the cold wood, pulled the hammer back, and lightly rested his finger on the trigger. As he looked down the barrel across the open iron sights, a sudden rush of melancholy washed over him. *Remember how this feels…memorize it!* he thought.

The loud and welcome report of the rifle was music to Merle's ears. But as the small lead bullet sped out of the muzzle, a cannon-ball of emotions entered his heart, exploding the dam in his soul that was holding back a river of tears.

It was a full minute before he could clearly see the deer that was lying on the flat below him. He quickly chambered another shell, carefully put the hammer down to the safety position, and took his binoculars from his pack. After wiping his eyes with his sleeve, he focused his field glasses on the deer's side. With no sign of up and down breathing movement, he cradled the Winchester in his arms and walked down the hill to the buck.

Standing over the sizable animal, Merle lifted Old Ironsights to his face, kissed it on the serial number, and said, "An eight-pointer, huh? You're trying to make this decision extra hard on me, aren't you?"

The climb required to hunt high at his favorite oak tree was rewarded with a relatively easy drag of the deer downhill to his

truck. On the way down, Merle had time to rehearse the conversation he would have with the fellow who had responded to the ad about the Winchester. He knew how much he needed to get for the gun to buy his three youngsters the gifts he'd chosen. Armed with that number, he audibly practiced holding out for his price. Though he had no plans of coming off the number, he wondered if he had subconsciously set the price so high that no one would make an acceptable offer. But a man had responded to the ad, so Merle knew it was probably a matter of his willingness to negotiate.

The eight-point caused quite a stir at the check-in station. Merle enjoyed the "atta boy" that his friends and neighbors offered. As he climbed into his truck to head home with his trophy, one of the hunters approached Merle.

"Did you get that deer with that .32 you're trying to sell?"

"Sure did. It's a fine rifle. I guess you saw the ad."

"I did. I'd take it off your hands right now if I had the funds. You wouldn't come down on the price, would you?"

Merle's rehearsal regarding his asking price made it easy to respond to the inquiry. "No, sir. I'm not negotiating. I don't want to insult a great gun!"

The stranger understood how deep feelings can go in a fellow's heart for his favorite deer rifle. He smiled at Merle's defense of his price and tipped his ball cap. He hopped into his truck and drove away.

Merle drove home, and after skinning the big buck and hanging it in his backyard shed, he went into the house to make the phone call he dreaded. His wife, Peggy, could hear his side of the conversation, and from what she could gather, she guessed that within a couple of hours they'd have a visitor. When he hung up she turned from the stove to look at him.

"Sounds like the buyer didn't balk at your price."

"I'm not sure why he wants my Winchester so much, but he didn't make a single attempt to challenge the price. He lives way over on

the other side of the county, so he said he'll be here around three. He asked me to hold the gun until then. I said I would."

Merle sipped his coffee as Peggy continued making breakfast.

"I may be one of a few women who understand your affection for that Winchester, Merle. My dad had a 12-gauge he was mighty fond of. I know in a hunter's mind, his gun is more than just meticulously crafted wood and steel. For Dad, it was a means for providing food, a protector, and, perhaps most important, that pump shotgun was a connection between him and something he felt he was really good at. And he was, as you know. Being one of the best hunters in these parts, Dad took care of that gun nearly as well as he cared for us kids. So, Mr. Merle, I know how hard this is for you. I know what it's taking out of you."

Merle smiled at Peggy but didn't comment.

"The reason you're selling that gun says a ton about you as a dad. I've never known a man who is as good a dad as you are, Merle. You're beyond amazing. Not many serious hunters I know would choose a good Christmas for their sons over their love of the sport. I love you for that, honey. And I'm proud of you." Tears welled up in her eyes as she walked over and gave Merle a hug. "And Merle, if you want to change your mind, it's okay. We can get by. The buyer probably hasn't left home yet."

Merle stood up holding his coffee cup. He walked to the window and looked outside toward the shed where the deer was. He stood there for a while, quietly sipping his brew.

"Peggy, you'll never know how much your words mean to me. I love you. I know the boys will be fine with that whatever happens Christmas morning, but I want this year to be extra special. Mike is old enough now for the pellet gun I want to get him, and Charles has been talking about that radio building kit he saw at the hardware store since last summer. Thomas has had a picture of that Navy ship model he's dreamed about tacked to the bottom of the bunk bed above him for I don't know how long.

"This doggone economic downturn sure came at a bad time. Maybe I'm letting it mess with my manhood, but I really want to see pure joy on the boys' faces when they open up their presents this year. Seeing and feeling their joy will trump any affection I feel for Old Ironsights."

"You're right about the boys," Peggy affirmed. "Christmas morning will be fun for them whatever happens. Besides, we both agree we want to be careful about sending them the wrong message about what Christmas is all about. We don't want them to focus on the gift giving as much as on 'The Gift' God gave us in His Son, Jesus. As long as we keep that fact first, the boys will be fine.

"But I can also see the twinkles in your eyes when you think about how excited the boys will be with their presents. I'll say it again, Merle. You're a good man—a very good man."

Eventually three o'clock arrived, and so did the potential buyer. Merle met him on the front porch of their little house and invited him in. He didn't offer small talk; he simply handed him the gun that was cleaned and packed in the original cardboard box.

The man pulled out the gun, looked it over carefully, and asked a few questions about its age and if there was anything he should know about it.

Merle offered a couple of tips on how to clean it and what grain of bullet worked best.

The man got up. "I'll take it." He handed Merle an envelope filled with cash and then packed the gun back into the box. He picked his purchase up, shook hands with Merle, said goodbye, and walked out the front door.

Merle watched him get into his truck and back out of the driveway. As a way of saying a respectful farewell to an old friend and a huge piece of his heart, Merle stood on the porch and watched the truck until it disappeared around a bend in the highway.

A few days later, funds in hand, Merle headed to the hardware store.

"Good morning, Merle. Merry Christmas to you and yours."

"And the same to you, Mr. Adams."

"Merle, I saw the ad you placed in the paper a couple of weeks ago. Was that .32 the same gun you bought here when you were a lad?"

"I'm amazed at how many people saw that ad. Yes, it was the same one." Merle sighed. "I'm thinking the entire world gets the paper."

"The price you put on that gun sure represented quite an appreciation in value."

"Truth is, Mr. Adams, it was a whole lot more valuable to me than the dollar figure I put on it. A fellow across the county wasn't deterred by my asking price. He came over and bought it a few days ago. And now I'm here to bless your business with the appreciation value. I'd better get to it."

With his mind on Christmas morning, Merle searched the store for the items on his list. He felt great as he picked out the presents, and he was really pleased when he had enough cash left to get Peggy the blender she'd drooled over the last time they were in the store together.

Christmas Day arrived. It was a glorious time. Merle's spirits were sailing high when his boys tore past the wrapping paper and found their gifts. The high-pitched squeals of excitement were followed by neck-breaking hugs of youthful thanks. Merle beamed and knew he'd received plenty of rewards for sacrificing his Winchester.

And when Peggy opened the blender, her oohs and aahs warmed his heart. Merle admitted that the morning had yielded even more joy than he imagined. However, though the room was electric with Christmas joy, for a passing moment Merle thought of Old Ironsights and wondered if his beloved gun was out hunting with a stranger. *I sure hope the new guy appreciates what he has.*

The following year the economy turned around a bit, and Merle's

business improved. Merle eventually purchased a new gun and continued to take his boys hunting even as they grew into their teens and into young adulthood.

Time passes like it always does, and soon the three boys were married and on their own. They often converged at the "old home place" to visit. The three boys often showed up together. Peggy was convinced they always smelled the fresh apple pies baking in her oven.

One morning just before Thanksgiving, while Merle was helping a friend with a house repair, the three boys sat at the kitchen table talking to their mom and, of course, eating pie. As they discussed the plans for the upcoming holidays, they also reminisced about Christmases past. All three of them readily agreed that one of their favorite memories centered around the wonderful year the gifts included the pellet gun, radio building kit, and model ship. They glowed with the warmth of the memories.

"Boys, do you know how that Christmas came about?" Peggy asked.

"What do you mean, Mom?"

"Let me tell you something about your dad. That particular year, times were pretty rough. The business was struggling, and the economy was down. Your dad was worried about Christmas and how he could make it especially memorable for you boys. He loves you so much, and that year he wanted your gifts to be extra special. The only way he could figure out how to get you the gifts you longed for was to sell his hunting rifle."

Peggy continued fleshing out the story, adding the pertinent details. She shared how their dad had saved his money as a teen to buy the rifle, and how much he'd loved taking Old Ironsights to the woods. "They were quite a team," Peggy said as she wrapped up the story.

The boys were silent for a long time. Finally Michael, the oldest, said, "That's an amazing story, Mom. I'm glad you told us about

Old Ironsights." He looked at his brothers. "We have a wonderful Dad, don't we?"

After the chorus of agreement, Michael continued, "Guys, I have an idea for something for Dad for Christmas. It might take some doing…and maybe even a God-given miracle, but here's what I'm thinking…" As Michael laid out his idea, his two brothers whole-heartedly agreed.

Christmas morning arrived, and in keeping with tradition, the entire family, including spouses, gathered at noon at Merle and Peggy's house. The collective excitement emanating from the three brothers was electric. In fact, the brothers could barely stand the suspense of knowing they'd found their dad a perfect and unique gift.

Michael, Charles, and Thomas finally announced, "Dad and Mom, this year we're going to do Christmas a little bit different. And Dad, you can't stop us. We want to exchange gifts *before* we eat lunch."

Before Merle could respond, Peggy responded. "That's fine with us, boys. No need to be in a rut. Let's do it."

Wrapping paper and ribbons flew as the family members took turns opening gifts. Per tradition, the youngest person opened a present, then the next youngest, and on up the age ladder. When all the gifts had been opened and it looked like it was time to dig into the delicious food simmering on the stove and in the oven, Michael spoke up.

"Dad, there's one more gift to open. It's a special present to you from us boys. We think you're going to really like it."

Charles got up and walked across the living room to the closet. Opening the door and digging way back inside behind the coats, he finally pulled out a rectangular box wrapped in dark green paper.

"It's heavy, Dad," he said as he handed it to Merle.

Merle smiled and looked at his family. "What have you boys done?" He slipped his fingers under the wrapping paper between

two tabs of Scotch tape and tore the paper back. A brown box with a large logo was exposed. He spelled the word out loud: "W-I-N-C-H-E-S-T-E-R."

Merle's eyes filled with tears as he grinned and stripped off the rest of the paper. Suddenly he stopped. He stared at the box, noting it's yellowed color and bent corners. He looked up. "I've seen this box before..." Carefully he lifted the lid and stared at the lone item inside.

"Old Ironsights. It's Old Ironsights! My first rifle!" Merle's grin rivaled the one on his face so many years ago when he'd paid Mr. Adams and took the gun home for the first time.

The grin was repeated on everyone's faces.

"Boys, I can't believe it! How did you know about this? And how did you track Old Ironsights down?"

"It wasn't easy, Dad," Thomas said. "Just before Thanksgiving Mom told us the story about what you did for us that Christmas so many years ago. We decided we would try to find the buyer and get your gun back. You didn't have a receipt, but Mom finally remembered enough about the man to get us started."

Michael added, "You might like to know that the fellow who bought the gun from you passed on seven or eight years ago. He left Old Ironsights to his son, who was willing to part with it. He drove a hard bargain, but we didn't hesitate. Mom told us what this .32 meant to you...and what it did for us. It would've been a sad Christmas if we didn't bring it back home."

"Did he beat you boys up really bad with his asking price?"

Charles chuckled. "Yep. Our wallets are bruised a little, mainly because of something he said. We stopped trying to negotiate when he said, 'I ain't dickerin' with you boys 'cause it just wouldn't be right to insult a great gun.' He told us his dad taught him that. So we went ahead and bit the economic bullet. Between the three of us we spread out the cost so it didn't put any of us in the poorhouse."

Thomas added, "At least he threw in two boxes of shells. They're in the closet on the shelf."

"Boys, you done good—real good. By the look on your dad's face, I'd say the outlay was worth it."

"Yes, ma'am," the three boys replied in unison.

The next morning the clock on Merle's side of the bed went off at three-thirty. Peggy roused, sat up, rubbed her eyes, and looked at the clock on her side of the bed. Then she looked at Merle.

"I'm sorry you woke up, Peggy," Merle said. "I was hoping you wouldn't."

"It's okay, Merle. No need to explain. I know why you're up so early. Be careful and enjoy the morning with your old friend."

"I love you, honey."

She couldn't see the smile on Merle's face in the darkness, but she knew it was there.

Merle parked his truck and climbed the hill toward the red oak. Though the ascent took longer and consumed more energy than it used to, he managed it in the predawn. He set up his portable chair, settled it next to the red oak, and sat down, leaning against the tree while cradling his rifle. He looked up to the sky that was showing more light. "Thank You, God, for this place and for letting me come back to it. And thanks for the fine sons You gave me. Can you believe what they did for me? They found Old Ironsights. And God, thank You for all You've done for me too."

He patted the stock of his .32. "Welcome home, Old Ironsights! It's time to get to huntin'!"

ABOUT STEVE CHAPMAN

Steve's love of hunting began in his early teens on a weekend when one of his dad's church members invited him to tag along on an October squirrel hunt. Archery is his first choice for use in the field, followed by muzzle loader, and then pistol or rifle. To date, according to Steve's calculations, he's entered the woods before daylight on over a thousand mornings and hopes to continue that trend for many more years!

Proudly claiming West Virginia as his home state, Steve grew up as the son of a preacher. He met his wife, Annie, in junior high school. Twelve years later they married after dating a few months and settled in Nashville, Tennessee, where they raised their son and daughter, Nathan and Heidi. When Nathan married Stephanie and Heidi married Emmitt, Steve and Annie enthusiastically accepted their new daughter-in-law and son-in-law, and now they get to dote on their grandchildren, Lily and Josie.

Steve is president of S&A Family, Inc., an organization formed to oversee the production of the Chapmans' recorded music. They've had "family life" as the theme of their lyrics since they began singing together. As Dove Award-winning artists, their schedule sends them to more than 100 cities a year to present concerts.

— More Great Books from —
Steve Chapman

10 Things I Want My Son to Know

365 Things Every Hunter Should Know

A Look at Life from a Deer Stand

A Look at Life from a Deer Stand Devotional

Another Look at Life from a Deer Stand

The Good Husband's Guide to Balancing Hobbies and Marriage

Hot Topics for Couples
(with Annie Chapman)

A Hunter's Call

A Hunter Sets His Sights

With God on a Deer Hunt

Gift Books

Fish Tales

A Look at Life from a Deer Stand Gift Edition

Pursuing the Prize

Quiet Moments for Your Soul
(with music CD by Heidi Chapman)

HARVEST HOUSE
PUBLISHERS

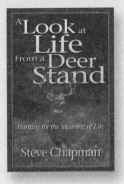

A LOOK AT LIFE FROM A DEER STAND

From the incredible rush of bagging "the big one" to standing in awe of God's magnificent creation, avid sportsman Steve Chapman captures the spirit of the hunt. In short chapters filled with excitement and humor, he takes you on his successful and not-so-successful forays into the heart of deer country. As you experience the joy of scouting a trophy buck, you'll discover how the skills necessary for great hunting can help you draw closer to the Lord.

ANOTHER LOOK AT LIFE FROM A DEER STAND

Drawing on his many years of hunting, Steve takes you to the forests and fields to experience the exhilaration of sighting whitetails and wily turkeys. From the joys of being in the woods to the thrill of handling well-made equipment, you'll relate to the adventure of going after wild game. Along the way you'll also garner some intriguing life truths that will impact your everyday life...spiritual truths that reflect the bounty and grace of the Creator.

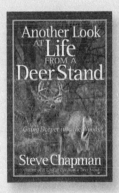

Steve's books are available
at your local Christian bookstores.

To read a sample chapter, go to www.harvesthousepublishers.com.

QUIET MOMENTS FOR YOUR SOUL

with "Hymns from God's Great Cathedral" CD
sung by Heidi Chapman Beall

Avid outdoorsman Steve Chapman encourages you to seek rest, comfort, and restoration in God's great cathedral. "There is a place for you to go to find solace," Steve writes. "Step outside...take your broken heart to the openness of the temple God has made."

Breathtaking photographs by John MacMurray provide windows to nature's sanctuary as Steve's personal stories and reflections help you stand on the shore of God's strength, climb the mountain peak under God's protection, and experience the comfort of God's creation.

This beautiful hardcover book extends its gift of comfort with an exclusive, accompanying CD, "Hymns from God's Great Cathedral," featuring the vocals of Steve's daughter, Heidi Chapman Beall.

Steve's books are available
at your local Christian bookstores.

To read a sample chapter, go to www.harvesthousepublishers.com.